Fast Track to **FCE**

CW00420125

Jane Allemano
Mary Stephens

Exam Practice
Workbook

Contents map

1 Entertainment

Vocabulary ▶ CB Reading 1 pp.4–5

1 Word formation

Use the correct form of the word in capitals at the end of each sentence to fill the gap.

1 Tom is a great artist; he's done some fantastic _drawings_ of the people in his class. **DRAW**
2 Who was the .... of the last Star Wars film? **DIRECTON**
3 The film they showed on TV last night was .... scary. **EXTREME**ly   _zakładnie!_
4 The government have set up an .... which helps young actors financially. **ORGANISE** ious
5 The play was .... written to celebrate the city's history. **SPECIAL**ly
6 I think they should cut the .... of the musical by about 30 minutes. **LONG** lenght

2 Choosing the right word

Underline the correct word from the options given in *italics*.

1 Films with well-known stars attract very large _audiences_/spectators.   kibice
siedzi w/ 2 The actor had trouble learning the *play/script* for
tylku i   the film.   aktor zawienia
ogląda co/ 3 The camera *crew/organisation* finished filming at midnight.
4 When they filmed *Titanic*, they built a special _set_/location in the studio.
5 It took them weeks to design and paint the *scene/scenery* for the film.
6 The *plot/theme* of *Romeo and Juliet* is love and hate.
fabuła + myśl przewodnia

3 Verb + noun collocations

Complete the collocations below with a verb from the list. The noun is in *italics* to help you.

~~achieve~~ / form / ~~hire~~ / ~~make~~ / pay / ~~play~~

1 That director is going to _make_ *a film* about the first Olympic Games.
2 Who is going to _play_ *the role* of James Bond in the next film?
3 That producer had problems at the start of her career but she went on to _achieve_ *success* later.
4 The actress refused to fly with the rest of the public so the producer had to _hire_ *a private plane* for her.
5 Do film companies have to _pay_ *tax* to the government if they want to film in your country?
6 The actors are tired of working for big studios so they are planning to _form_ *their own company* and produce films themselves.

Grammar and Use of English

▶ CB pp.6–7, grammar files 4, 5

1 Present simple or present continuous?

Put the verbs in brackets into the correct tense, present simple or present continuous.

1 What _do you think_ (you/think) of the latest Bond movie?
2 Shh! Don't disturb Sam. He .... (read) a thriller.
3 I .... (not/understand) the plot of this film. The hero .... (fly) across the world and .... (go) through all sorts of danger to find the woman he .... (love). But when he .... (find) her, he .... (decide) he .... (not/like) her!
4 I .... (think) of buying a video. Which would you recommend?
5 My brother .... (train) to be an actor.
6 That art exhibition .... (sound) really good.
7 My sister annoys me because she _is always talking_ (always/talk) about herself!
8 How _do you_ (you/feel) about horror movies?
9 My favourite group .... (appear) at a local theatre tonight.
10 I'm _working_ (work) in a theatre for a month as part of my college course.

2 Adverbs of frequency

grammar file

A Position of adverbs

We use adverbs of frequency such as:
always, often, usually, sometimes, occasionally, hardly ever (= almost never), seldom, rarely, never:

● after simple tenses of the verb *to be*:
  *He is **usually** late.*

● before simple tenses of all other verbs:
  *They **hardly ever** go to the cinema.*

● after the first auxiliary verb in complex tenses:
  *I have **always** seen really good films at the festival.*

Adverbs such as: *every day, twice a day, now and again, most days* go at the beginning or end of the sentence:
*I go to the library after school **most days**.*

B Negative adverbs

Adverbs with a negative meaning are accompanied by a positive verb:
*I **hardly ever** go to the cinema (= I **don't often** go to the cinema.)*

harnet — oxere2ou

Find the mistake in each sentence below, and rewrite the sentences correctly.

1 Often I play the drums in a local band.
I often play the drums in a local band. ....

2 I have been never to a film studio before.
I have never been to a film studio ....

3 I've got a video but I don't have ~~usually~~ enough time to watch it.
....

4 My sister always has wanted to be an actress.
...*has always wanted to be* ....

5 We ~~go~~ rarely to the theatre but we go now and again to the cinema.
...*but we are going to the cinema again* ...

6 They don't show usually rock concerts on television.
....

7 I never have seen a horror movie before.
....

8 My brother always is complaining about TV programmes but he still watches them!
....

pize bidum ou *zakolowo* *2 cpus*

3 *will* **or present continuous?**

Underline the correct tense from the options given in *italics*.

1 My favourite rock group *will come/is coming* to this town next week.

2 'Oh no! There's a great film on TV tonight and *we'll go/we're going* out. *We'll miss/We're missing* it!'
'Never mind, *I'm videoing/I'll video* it for you.'

3 Oh, look – he's a well-known actor! *Am I asking/ Shall I ask* him for his autograph?

4 I don't feel very well today. I don't think *I'm going/ I'll go* to the theatre after all.

5 I've promised *I'm getting/I'll get* my brother tickets for a musical for his birthday.

6 'Look! They *will show/are showing* Titanic on TV tonight!'
'Are they? In that case, I think *I'm staying/I'll stay* at home!'

4 *will* **or** *going to?* *Homework*

Put the verbs in brackets into the correct form.

1 Look at the clouds! It *is going to rain* (rain).

2 We .... (visit) a film studio tomorrow. It's all arranged.

3 'I must phone the theatre and book some tickets.'
'I .... (do) that for you, shall I?'

4 I .... (be) an actor when I leave school. I decided last week.

5 .... (you/see) the new art exhibition next week?

6 Don't worry about getting to the theatre tomorrow.
I .... (drive) you if you like!

grammar file

Other ways of referring to the future

We can use these verbs or phrases to talk about the future: *be likely/unlikely to, be bound to* and *be due to.*

1 *It's* **likely to** rain. (= It will probably rain.)

2 *He's* **unlikely to** visit us. (= He probably won't visit us.)

3 *They're* **bound to** enjoy the concert. (= They will certainly enjoy the concert.)

4 *The train is* **due to** arrive at 8. (= The train is scheduled to arrive at 8.)

5 **Transformations**

Complete the second sentence so that it has a similar meaning to the first sentence, using the word given. Do not change the word given. You must use between two and five words, including the word given.

1 I think John will definitely win the competition.
bound
John ....*is bound to win*...... the competition.

2 The band is just going to start playing.
about
The band .... playing.

3 A well-known actor will probably play the hero in the film.
likely
A well-known actor .... the hero in the film.

4 We've arranged to meet outside the cinema.
going
We .... outside the cinema.

5 I lose things all the time, which is really irritating!
am
I ...., which is really irritating!

6 The concert should start at 8.30 p.m., according to the schedule.
due
The concert .... 8.30 p.m.

7 We probably won't finish our work until tomorrow.
unlikely
We .... our work until tomorrow.

8 I'm sure they'll enjoy the concert.
bound
They .... the concert.

9 The film is unlikely to be a success.
probably
The film .... a success.

10 You are bound to get seats if you book in advance.
certainly
You .... if you book in advance.

Vocabulary ▶ CB Reading 2 pp.10–11

1 **Word formation** _HW_

Use the correct form of the word in capitals at the end of each sentence to fill the gap.

1 The book was full of wonderful, colour _illustrations_.
   ILLUSTRATE
2 The art gallery is under new _management_ . **MANAGE**
3 He's a millionaire and he owns a huge _collection_ of paintings. **COLLECT**
4 Thieves destroyed the sculpture without any _thinking_ of its value. **THINK**
5 We had a long _discussion_ about modern art. **DISCUSS**
6 I see you've decorated your room – I really like your _choice_ of posters. **CHOOSE**
7 I went to an art _exhibition_ in the Town Hall. **EXHIBIT**
8 I have no _intentions_ of studying Art next year. **INTEND**

2 **Verb + noun collocations** _HW_

▶▶ *exam tip!*

In **Paper 3**, **Part 1**, your knowledge of common collocations is often tested. When you add items to your vocabulary book, remember to include the words they collocate with.

Complete the collocations below with a verb from the list. The noun is in *italics* to help you.

join / keep / offer / solve / take

1 I think I'll _take_ *the Art Club* they've started in school. I really enjoy painting.
2 It will _offer_ *some time* to get the studio ready for the show.
3 The teacher tried to _offer_ Marco *some advice* on his painting technique but he wouldn't listen.
4 I've won a painting competition but I haven't told anyone yet – can you _keep_ *it a secret* for now?
5 It was difficult to move the sculpture but they managed to _solve_ *the problem* by getting a crane to lift it.

Vocabulary and Use of English

▶ CB pp.12–13

1 **Phrasal verbs with *get***

Complete the sentences below with a phrasal verb from the box in the correct form. Use the definitions in brackets to help you.

~~get on with~~   get at   get away with
get down to   get out of   get over

1 How are you _getting on with_ (= *progressing*) your painting?
2 Maria still hasn't _get over_ (= *recovered from*) the shock of winning that painting competition.
3 The thieves _get away with_ (= *escaped with*) some very valuable paintings.
4 We've got an art class this afternoon but I'm going to try to _get out of_ (= *avoid going to*) it.
5 The art teacher is always _get at_ (= *saying unkind things to*) me!
6 I'm so busy – I never have time to _get down to_ (= *seriously begin*) doing any of my hobbies.

2 **Linking expressions**

▶▶ *exam tip!*

In **Paper 3**, **Part 1**, you may be tested on your knowledge of linking words. It is important to learn how these words are used.

Read the information in the box, then do the exercise on page 7.

Linking words and expressions

A **Purpose and result**

1 *Because/As/Since* it was raining, the match was cancelled.
2 The match was cancelled **because of/on account of/due to** the rain.
3 It was raining. **Because of that,/Consequently,/As a result,** the match was cancelled.

B **Contrast**

1 *Although/Though/Even though* Jack is a good actor, he can't find a job.
2 *In spite of/Despite being* a good actor, Jack can't find a job.
3 Jack is a good actor. **Nevertheless,/However,/Yet** he can't find a job.
4 *Whereas/While* Jack is a good actor, he can't find a job.

**Complete the sentences below
with the correct word or phrase.
Use each word or phrase once only.**

pomimo że   powyżej że
| although | in spite of | *wzglos żać* |

1 *Although* my brother likes
   violent computer games, he is
   not an aggressive person.
2 Mum only lets him play for one hour
   each day, ... all his protests.

jednakże   podczas
| However | While |

3 My friends hate the theatre.
   However...., I think it's great.
4 .... I can't afford to go to
   the theatre very often, I often watch
   plays on the TV.

także i
| also | too |

5 We're going to see the new musical
   – are you coming ..*too*........ ?
6 We're going to a museum tomorrow
   and we're ..*also*..... hoping to visit
   an art gallery, if we have time.

| so | as |

7 The film had great reviews
   ..*so*........ I decided to see it.
8 I couldn't follow the plot very well
   ...*as*........ I'd missed the beginning
   of the film.

*żaden   żaden
ani jeden ani
drugi*
| neither | either |

9 .... of my parents knows
   much about modern art.
10 I don't think ..*either*... of them
   ever studied Art at school.

pomimo że   jednakże, ale
| Despite | Nevertheless |

11 The actors gave a great
   performance. *N*..........., the play
   did not get very good reviews.
12 *D*........... all their efforts, the
   actors could not stop the producer
   from closing the theatre.

**Read the text below and decide which answer A, B, C or D best
fits each space. There is an example at the beginning (0).**

0 A lead   B force   C guide   D make

MOVIE VIOLENCE

Some people think that movies can (0) *D* people violent. (1) .....,
I don't agree. I just don't believe that nice people become villains
after (2) ..... a film. Have any of *your* friends changed (3) .....
personality after watching a James Bond movie? I'm sure they
haven't!

In the early days of the cinema, critics (4) ..... that movies were
immoral and that they would destroy society. Teachers used to
(5) ..... their students from watching gangster films. They said
the students would all become gangsters (6) ..... they stopped
watching (7) ..... violent films immediately!

Things haven't altered a (8) ..... deal since then; people still
believe that movies make people violent. (9) ..... months ago,
our newspapers were full of (10) ..... about a violent criminal.
This criminal (11) ..... a terrible crime. Some reporters said the
man had become violent (12) ..... of watching a video called
Rambo. But it was later revealed that the man didn't own a
video player and had probably never (13) ..... seen *Rambo*.

I agree we need rules about what can be shown in the cinema.
But I hope the day never comes when we can (14) ..... longer
see gangster movies and action films (15) ..... *James Bond* in
our cinemas.

1	A	Despite	B	Although	C	However	D	Even though
2	A	looking	B	glimpsing	C	glancing	D	watching
3	A	a	B	their	C	the	D	his
4	A	said	B	told	C	meant	D	proposed
5	A	discourage	B	persuade	C	insist	D	deny
6	A	unless	B	provided	C	if	D	on condition
7	A	so	B	this	C	such	D	such a
8	A	large	B	huge	C	great	D	big
9	A	Some	B	Few	C	Little	D	Much
10	A	histories	B	stories	C	legends	D	myths
11	A	made	B	achieved	C	acted	D	committed
12	A	as a result	B	owing	C	due	D	for
13	A	just	B	even	C	only	D	after
14	A	any	B	much	C	not	D	no
15	A	as	B	such	C	similar	D	like

Answers marked: 1 C (However), 2 D (watching), 3 B (their), 4 A (said), 5 A (discourage), 6 A (unless), 7 C (such), 8 C (great), 9 B (Few), 10 B (stories), 11 D (committed), 13 B (even), 14 D (no), 15 A (as)

Reading: *multiple matching (headings)*

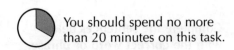

You should spend no more than 20 minutes on this task.

You are going to read a newspaper article about the history of board games. Choose the most suitable heading from the list **A–I** for each part (**1–7**) of the article. There is one extra heading which you do not need to use. There is an example at the beginning (**0**).

A   Instant access to a worldwide audience

B   Attempts at international organisation

C   Comparison with rival attractions

D   A combination of ideas

E   Earlier examples uncovered

F   A gathering of like-minded people

G   Reasons to think that interest is growing

H   A typical pattern of events

I   An important initial discovery

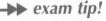 **exam strategy**   Paper 1, Part 1 ▶ CB p.10

▶▶ **exam tip!**
Look for words in the headings that paraphrase ideas and expressions in the text.

CLUES

Question:

2   This paragraph refers to the joining up of two different games. Look for a word in the headings which expresses this idea.

3   Look for a phrase in the headings which expresses the idea that games have 'all developed in a similar way'.

5   Examples are given to show the rising popularity of the games. Which heading expresses this idea?

6   Which heading combines the idea of a 'following' and 'people who share an enthusiasm'?

Power Play

Games have been played since the dawn of civilisation. As society progressed, so did the complexity of games.

0 /

In 1923, when a British archaeologist, Sir Leonard Woolley, excavated an archaeological site at Ur in Mesopotamia, he <u>discovered</u> five sets of a board game which <u>had first</u> been played around 5,000 years ago. Known as the Royal Game of Ur, this game is usually quoted as the <u>earliest</u> known board game. It was played in a similar way to modern board games, such as Ludo or Backgammon, with pieces being moved into, along and off the board according to the throw of pyramid-shaped dice.

1

Amazingly, more recent archaeological discoveries in Palestine and Jordan may make the Royal Game of Ur a relative newcomer. Game boards have been found that can be dated back to Neolithic times, some 4,000 years before the Royal Game of Ur. Indeed, it seems that certain civilisations actually developed board games before they could create pottery or even write.

2

Evidence from more recent times shows the development of games which demanded skill, logic and reason, not simply the lucky throw of dice. The ancient Greeks had a game called *petteia* which is mentioned in ancient texts. The game spread eastwards with the expansion of the Greek empire under Alexander the Great from about 330BC. It was the merging of this Greek game of reason with the ancient Indian game of chance called *chaturanga* that led to the development of the game we now know as Chess.

3

Major games like chess have all developed in a similar way. First of all, an originator comes up with a new, creative idea for a game which tests mental skills. This is then introduced to a wider range of players who form clubs. Champions then emerge who become the recognised leaders, experts and theorists of the game. This leads to formal competitions, literature and established game rules. The final stage is that national and international competitions arise, and a World Champion is crowned.

4

A natural limitation to the growth of 'mind games' in the past has been the fact that in most instances the number of players is two, occasionally three or four, and rarely more. Unlike a physical sporting event, the small size of the board usually limits the number of spectators to a handful. Contrast this with the number of people in a modern sports stadium and we can easily see why physical sports have been more popular than mental games as spectator events.

5

Despite these limiting barriers to the spread of mind sports as spectator events, the expansion in recent years has been staggering. A measure of the rising popularity of mind sports is reflected in the increased prize money offered to the winners of contests. And that's not all, the number of local, national and international competitions is increasing, whilst virtually all important newspapers and magazines run articles, columns and feature sections on Chess, Bridge and other brain-twisters.

6

In recent years, the annual Mind Sports Olympiad, an event held in London, has begun to attract a huge following. Eight thousand people who share an enthusiasm for such activities come together to take part in games such as Scrabble, Go, Chess, Bridge, Backgammon and the ancient African game Oware, probably the oldest board game still being actively played.

7

Competition on the mental battlefield can also be seen instantaneously via the Internet. In 1997, when Gary Kasparov, the famous Russian chess champion, played IBM's Deep Blue computer, the final hour of the final game attracted 22 million spectators around the world. Games have become far more than just a game – the future looks to be more challenging than ever.

Grammar ▶ CB p.15, grammar files 6, 8

1 Present perfect or past simple?

Put the verbs in brackets into the correct tense.

1 I _have always been_ (always/be) interested in the history of the cinema.
2 Last year, I .... (act) in several school plays.
3 That play ...... (just/open). Shall we go and see it?
4 How many times .... (you/watch) the video before you .... (give) it back?
5 I'd love to be an actor, but so far I.......... (never/have) the chance to appear on stage.
6 *Hamlet* is the most difficult play I .... (ever/read).

2 Present perfect simple or continuous?

Underline the correct tense from the options given in *italics*.

1 We *have rehearsed/have been rehearsing* for six months and we're still not ready!
2 Carlos is only 16 and he *has already starred/ has already been starring* in ten major films.
3 That film studio *has just closed/has just been closing* down.
4 Look at the queue outside the theatre! Those people *have waited/have been waiting* for hours!
5 That producer *has just won/has just been winning* two Oscars for his latest film.
6 I'm exhausted! We *have filmed/have been filming* since six o'clock this morning and we're still not finished.

3 Correct the mistakes

Two of the sentences below are correct. Tick them (✓). The other sentences contain tense errors. Underline the mistakes and correct them.

1 Last week I <u>have phoned</u> the theatre to book tickets. _phoned_
2 We have painted all the scenery and now we're going to have a break. ....

3 The actress is exhausted because she filmed for the last six hours. ....
4 We have queued for ages to get tickets yesterday. ....
5 Miguel says that this is the most dangerous job he ever did in his life. ....
6 Harry has written six novels so far and now he is working on the next one. ....

4 Transformations

Complete the second sentence so that it has a similar meaning to the first sentence, using the word given. Do not change the word given. You must use between two and five words, including the word given.

1 The actress began working in television in 1999. **been**
The actress _has been working_ in television since 1999.
2 How long have you been training to be a dancer? **start**
When .... to be a dancer?
3 The play only started a couple of minutes ago so we haven't missed much. **just**
The play .... so we haven't missed much.
4 The ballet company are just finishing a six-month tour. **for**
The ballet company .... six months.
5 The actors started rehearsing two months ago. **been**
The actors .... two months.
6 It's almost a year since I last went to the cinema. **for**
I .... the cinema for almost a year.
7 I have never seen such a terrible film before. **ever**
This is the worst film .... seen.
8 Tom has never acted in public before. **first**
This is the .... acted in public.
9 The theatre was last used a year ago. **for**
The theatre .... a year.
10 The theatre first became important in ancient times. **since**
The theatre .... ancient times.

Writing: *formal letter of application*

▶ **CB pp.14–15**

1 **1 Read the exam task and answer the questions below.**

You see this advertisement on a school noticeboard:

> **Theatre summer school**
> **1–6 August**
>
> Courses in acting, directing, costume, set design, make-up, lighting.
>
> A big final production at the end of the week.
>
> Total cost £540 (accommodation provided).
>
> To apply, please write to James Black giving details of previous experience and areas of interest.

Write a letter of application for this course. Write your letter in 120–180 words in an appropriate style. Do not write any postal addresses.

1 Who is James Black?
   a) a student
   b) an actor
   c) the course organiser
2 What style should you use to write this letter?
   a) informal   b) formal

2 Read the advertisement again and underline the points you need to bear in mind when you write your letter. Which of the following points must you include in the task? Tick them. Which can you include if you want? Put ? next to them.

1 what you have done in the theatre
2 why you want to do the course
3 which parts of the course you are interested in
4 what other information you would like to have about the course

2 **Read the following letter of application to the theatre summer school.**

1 Complete the letter by choosing the more suitable expression a) or b) from 1–10 below.

(1) ......*a)*........

(2) .... your advertisement in the Evening Standard for a summer theatre school. (3) .... as I would like to make a career in the theatre. I am 18 years old and I am finishing school this summer. I have studied drama at school and (4) .... I have taken part in several school productions not only as an actor but also helping with lighting and costumes. (5) .... I have never done any directing and I hope this course will give me the opportunity to do so. (6) .... the options, (7) .... giving me some more information about what is included in the lighting course as I already have some experience and (8) .... something new. I would also be interested in set design because I think it would help me with lighting.

(9) ....

(10) ....

Bob Stevens

1 a) Dear Mr Black	b) Dear Course Director
2 a) A friend showed me	b) I am writing in response to
3 a) It looks great	b) I am interested in applying,
4 a) it has always been my favourite subject	b) I think it's great
5 a) One of my regrets is that	b) What a pity
6 a) About	b) Regarding
7 a) how about	b) would you mind
8 a) I would like to learn	b) I'm really keen to learn
9 a) I look forward to hearing from you.	b) Please write soon.
10 a) Best wishes,	b) Yours sincerely,

2 Match the phrases in the gaps to the following functions.

a) why you want to do the course .....
b) formal ending .....
c) closing the letter .....
d) reason for writing .....
e) formal greeting ..*1*..
f) request for information .....

3 **The letter is written as one paragraph, which would lose marks in the exam. Mark with a / where there should be a new paragraph.**

2 Challenges

[handwritten: zaniespodnienkawowany]

[handwritten: z nobilem / nobilem]

Vocabulary ▶ CB Reading 1 pp.16–17

1 Word formation

1 Use the correct form of the word in capitals at the end of each sentence to fill the gap.

1 They risked their lives on expeditions which were often .... dangerous. **CREDIBLE** *[handwritten: incredibly]*
2 The men who were in charge of these expeditions needed good .... skills. **LEADER** *[handwritten: leaderships]*
3 Explorers like Shackleton and Cook had great .... of character. **STRONG** *[handwritten: strength]*
4 These great explorers had to face .... dangers and hardships. **IMAGINABLE** *[handwritten: unimaginable]*
5 They had to cope with many problems, both physical and .... **PSYCHOLOGY**
6 They remained cheerful and never lost their .... **OPTIMISTIC** *[handwritten: optimizm]*

2 Prepositional phrases

Complete the phrases in *italics* with a word from the list.

spirits / hope / display / danger / horror
[handwritten numbers: 3 / 2 / 5 / 4 / 1]

1 The explorers were sailing to Antarctica when, *to their* ...., their ship became trapped in ice.
2 They stayed on the ship, *in the* .... that the ice would soon melt.
3 The captain tried to keep his crew *in good* .... by organising games and activities.
4 They walked over the ice to a nearby island, but they were still *in* .... of starving to death.
5 Today, the ship is *on* .... in a museum.

3 Verb + preposition collocations

Fill the gaps with a preposition from the list.

about / from / to

1 There was no water so the members of the expedition *suffered* ...*from*... thirst.
2 The sailors tried not to *think* ...*about*... the dangers of their situation.
3 The explorers' special clothing *saved them* ...*from*... the intense cold.
4 We tried to make radio contact with the men, but they did not *respond* ...*to*... any of our signals.

Grammar and Use of English

▶ CB pp.18–19, grammar files 6, 8

1 Past simple or past continuous?

Read the text, then put the verbs in brackets into the correct tense.

Tom (1) ...*was having*.. (have) a ten-minute break from his boring office job, when he (2) ...*saw*.......... (see) an interesting advertisement in a magazine. Some people (3) ...*were* ...*ing*... (plan) to sail around the world. They (4) ...*were* ...*ing*.. (look) for another member of the crew for their boat. Tom (5) .... (sigh) *[handwritten: ed]* and (6) ...*looked*..... (look) around his office. Everyone (7) ...*was*.............. (type) letters and the phones (8) ...*were*....... (ring), just as they (9) ...*did*........ (do) every day. He (10) ...*was* ...*ing*... (think) about the advertisement for a long time. He knew that he (11) ...*did not*....... (not/want) to spend his whole life working in a job like this one. He (12) ...*was* ...*ing*. (still/think) about the advertisement when his boss (13) ...*came*....... (come) along and (14) ...*gave*........ (give) him lots more boring work to do. 'Right,' he (15) ...*decided*... (decide), 'I'm definitely going to answer that advert. Sailing around the world would be much more interesting than this!'

For Exercises **2**–**5**, underline the correct tense from the options given in *italics*.

2 Past simple or past perfect?

1 The explorers *already climbed/had already climbed* a long way up the mountain when it *suddenly started/had suddenly started* to snow heavily.
2 When one of the climbers *saw/had seen* that her friend was in trouble, she *ran/had run* to help him.
3 By the time the climbers *reached/had reached* the top of the mountain, the sun *disappeared/had disappeared*.

[handwritten: zaizu]

3 Past perfect simple or continuous?

1 The men wanted to discover lands that nobody else
had explored/had been exploring yet.
2 The men were sad because they *had left/had been
leaving* their families and friends at home.
3 The mountaineer was exhausted when he returned
to the camp, because he *had climbed/had been
climbing* all morning.
4 After two months at sea, they *had eaten/had been
eating* nearly all of their food supplies.

4 Past continuous or past perfect continuous?

1 The men *were only diving/had only been diving* for
ten minutes when they found the buried treasure. *skarb*
2 They found the wrecked ship while they *were
exploring/had been exploring* the island.
3 When they returned to their ship, their friends *were
waiting/had been waiting* for them.
4 The ship *was lying/had been lying* at the bottom of
the sea for 200 years before they found it.

5 Past tenses

Antonio and his friend Pietro (1) *had lain/had been
lying* on the beach for about an hour when they heard
somebody shouting. They (2) *were jumping up/jumped
up* and saw that there was a man in trouble in the sea.
The man (3) *had been catching/had caught* his foot
between two rocks. He (4) *was trying/had been trying* to
free himself for quite a long time, but without success.
The friends realised that the man (5) *was drowning/had
been drowning* and that they needed to act quickly
to save him. Without thinking, they (6) *jumped/were
jumping* into the sea. When they reached the man, they
(7) *had dived/dived* underwater. After they (8) *were
struggling/had been struggling* for several seconds, they
managed to free the man. They (9) *were swimming/swam*
back to the shore, and pulled the man between them.
By the time they reached the beach, many people
(10) *gathered/had gathered* there, and everyone started
to clap and cheer. *wiwatować*

6 Transformations

**Complete the second sentence so that it has a similar
meaning to the first sentence, using the word given.
Do not change the word given. You must use between
two and five words, including the word given.**

1 During the journey to Australia, they saw many
uninhabited islands. **while**
They saw many uninhabited islands *while they were
travelling to* Australia.
2 She was excited because it was her first trip to Africa.
never
She was excited because *she has never been to*
Africa before.

3 Their flight was ten hours long, so they were
exhausted when they arrived. **for** *widoczny efekt*
When they arrived, they were exhausted because
they *have been flying for* ten hours.
4 When the sky became dark, the explorers hadn't yet
climbed the mountain. **still**
The sky became dark while the explorers
were still climbing the mountain.
5 He saw many temples during his job in India. **while**
He saw many temples *while he was working in*
India.
6 He hasn't done any climbing for 20 years. **did**
It's 20 years *since he did* any climbing.
7 He phoned me on his arrival in Antarctica. **soon**
He phoned me *as soon as arrived* in
Antarctica.
8 It was their first flight. **had**
They *had never flown* before.
9 I haven't been to France since I was a child. **when**
I last *was in France when* I was a child.
10 They haven't travelled abroad for ages. **since**
It's ages *since they were* abroad.

7 Auxiliary verbs

> **exam tip!**
>
> In **Paper 3**, **Part 2**, there may be gaps which are
> followed by present participles (-*ing* forms)
> or past participles (-*ed* forms). You may have to
> fill the gap with one of the following auxiliary verbs:
> - *am/is/are/was/were/been* + -*ing*
>   (= continuous tenses)
> - *has/have/had* + -*ed/past participle*
>   (= perfect tenses)
> - *am/are/was/were/been* + -*ed/past participle*
>   (= passive tenses)

**Fill the gaps in these sentences with the correct
auxiliary verb. Use the words in *italics* to help you.**

1 The islands *were* discovered *in 1897*.
2 *During the past few years*, several people *have* sailed
around the world single-handed.
3 *By the time* they left camp, it *had* started to snow.
4 He *had* been sailing *for some weeks by the time* he
finally saw land. *zanim*
5 They played cards *while* they *were* waiting.
6 The explorer *was* found by a team of rescuers *late last
night*.
7 The climbers *have* just finished their meal and *now*
they are ready to go.
8 The explorer *has* not reached the South Pole *yet* but
he will.

8 Structural cloze

Read the text below and think of the word which best fits each space. Use only one word in each space. There is an example at the beginning (0).

THE OREGON TRAIL

In the early 19th century an amazing thing happened in America. Nearly half a million people left their homes and headed West along what (0) ...*was*... called 'the Oregon Trail', a path across the country to California and Oregon. What made them set out on this epic journey across sweltering hot deserts, fast-flowing rivers and high mountains? The men and women who risked their lives to cross these wild and dangerous regions (1) ...were... called 'settlers'. They (2) ...were... escaping from poverty and hardship in the East and they (3) ...were... all looking for a new beginning and a better life in the West.

How (4) ...did... they find out about the opportunities that existed in the West? It seems that travellers who (5) ...have... been there on trading expeditions brought back stories of warmer winters and of good farming land that (6) ...was... being given away by the government. Then, in 1849, news came that men (7) ...had... just discovered gold in California.

By the early 1850s, people (8) ...were... rushing to reach the West. Some settlers could ride because they (9) ...had... bought horses, but most of them had to walk. On the journey, they met many dangers. They (10) ...were... crossing land that was mostly desert, so there was very little food or water. They (11) ...were... often attacked by the Indians who lived in those territories and they (12) ...were... also threatened by dangerous animals like snakes, and herds of wild buffalo. There was a serious danger of illness, and many settlers (13) ...did... not reach the West alive. But change (14) ...was... coming to the American West. By 1870, a new railway (15) ...had... been completed and the Oregon Trail had become a part of history.

Oregon Trail

Vocabulary ▶ CB Reading 2 pp.22–23

1 Verbs of movement

1 Match a word in column A with its meaning in column B.

A		B	
1	collapsed e	a)	got into/through a small space with difficulty
2	emerged g	b)	climbed, with difficulty
3	squeezed a	c)	hung from a string or rope
4	waded h	d)	moved very smoothly
5	clambered b	e)	fell down, exhausted
6	dangled c	f)	walked in a relaxed way
7	strolled f	g)	came out
8	glided d	h)	walked through deep water

2 Now fill the gaps in the sentences below using words from column A. The words in *italics* will help you to decide which word fits best.

1 Sonya ...*squeezed*... *through a tiny gap* in the rocks.
2 The skaters 8 .... *gracefully* across the ice.
3 To Paolo's horror, he found himself 6 .... *from a rope* above a deep valley.
4 The men 2 .... *from* the cave, blinking in the sunlight.
5 Ben 4 .... across *the shallow stream.*
6 They 7 .... *slowly* through the park.
7 He lost consciousness and 1 .... *onto the floor.*
8 Maria 5 .... *up the slippery rocks.*

2 Verb + noun collocations

Match a word in column A with a word in column B to form collocations. Then replace the words in *italics* in the sentences below with an appropriate collocation. Make any necessary changes.

A		B	
1	acquire	a)	a go at
2	have	b)	a new skill
3	lose	c)	attention (to something)
4	make	d)	friends
5	pay	e)	my/your/his nerve
6	take	f)	turns

1 I want to *try* canoeing on the adventure trip because I've never done it before. ...*have a go at*...
2 If you want to *learn how to do something new,* why not learn to abseil? ...1...
3 *Listen carefully* to what the instructor tells you. ...5...
4 If you go on an adventure holiday, I'm sure you'll *meet new people you like.* ...4...
5 Only one person can go down the climbing rope at a time, so you'll all have to *do it one after the other.* ...6...
6 I was going to try bungee-jumping, but I *got too frightened.* ...3...

Vocabulary and Use of English ▶ CB pp.24–25

1 Word formation

Study the information in the box, then do the exercise below.

Forming adjectives

● Adjectives are often formed with suffixes in this way:

verb + **-able**	e.g. break**able**, like**able**
noun + **-ful/less**	e.g. hope**ful**, help**less**
noun + **-ic**	e.g. hero**ic**, roman**tic**
noun + **-al**	e.g. sensation**al**, occasion**al**
noun + **-ous**	e.g. danger**ous**, carnivor**ous**
noun + **-ible**	e.g. terr**ible**, horr**ible**
noun + **-ent**	e.g. intellig**ent**, impati**ent**
noun + **-y**	e.g. rain**y**, angr**y**

● We can make adjectives negative by adding a prefix:

il- + **l** = **il**logical, **il**legal
ir- + **r** = **ir**responsible, **ir**regular
im- + **m/p** = **im**mature, **im**possible
un/in = **un**attractive, **in**comprehensible

Use the correct form of the word in capitals at the end of each sentence to fill the gap.

1 It's very *irresponsible* to go climbing without a helmet, because you could get badly hurt. **RESPONSIBLE**

2 My brother is a fantastic swimmer but he's .... at diving. **HOPE** *LESS*

3 It's not *sensibly* to go swimming after a heavy meal because you could drown. **SENSE**

4 Don't be so .... I'll be ready in a minute. **PATIENCE** *impatient*

5 My sister is not very .... about the idea of an adventure holiday. *enthusiastic* **ENTHUSIASM**

6 It was such a .... day that we couldn't go out at all. **RAIN**

7 The climber broke his leg and was .... of walking without help. *in***CAPABLE** *of*

8 That man was very .... when he ran to help the drowning boy without thinking of his own safety. **COURAGE***ous*

2 Word formation

1 Read the text below and <u>underline</u> which type of word is missing from the options given in brackets.

2 Now fill in the missing words. Use the word given in capitals below the text to form a word that fits in the space in the text. There is an example at the beginning (0).

ADVENTURE HOLIDAYS

Adventure holidays are popular because they offer plenty of (0) *excitement.* (<u>noun</u>/adjective). They are great fun, but can be very challenging. They give (1) .... (noun/<u>adjective</u>) teenagers a chance to take part in many sporting (2) *activitie* (<u>noun</u>/adjective). If you take an adventure holiday, make sure that all of your (3) .... (<u>noun</u>/adjective) are experienced. If you discover that any of the staff are (4) *unqualified* (verb/<u>adjective</u>), do not go out with them. Check the centre provides all the (5) *safety* ... (noun/<u>adjective</u>) equipment that you need. Helmets and torches, which may seem (6) *unnecessary* (<u>adjective</u>/adverb) *annoying* and pointless can make the difference between life and (7) *death* ... (<u>noun</u>/adjective) if there is an accident. Remember that although activities sound very (8) *attractive* (<u>adjective</u>/adverb) in a book or on TV, they may be much less fun in (9) *reality* (<u>noun</u>/adverb). Bungee-jumping is an incredible experience, but also very (10) .... (adjective/<u>adverb</u>). If you find at the last moment that you are really terrified, then don't do it!

---

(0) **EXCITE**	(4) **QUALIFY**	(8) **ATTRACT**
(1) **ENERGY** *energetic*	(5) **SAFE**	(9) **REAL**
(2) **ACTIVE**	(6) **NECESSARY**	(10) **FRIGHTEN** *ing*
(3) **INSTRUCT** *ORS*	(7) **DIE**	

Reading: *multiple-choice questions*

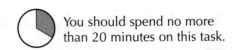

You should spend no more than 20 minutes on this task.

You are going to read a magazine article about the adventure sport called bungee-jumping. For questions 1–7, choose the answer (**A, B, C** or **D**) which you thinks fits best according to the text.

Living Dangerously

People cross continents to bungee-jump off the Victoria Falls in Africa

Bungee-jumping is not new. Millions of people have jumped from high places with elastic tied to their ankles, but until recently, not me. There are plenty of places to try a jump, some no great distance from my home. Unlike my friends, however, I was looking for a better view than that from a crane in a London suburb, so I chose one of the world's classic bungee locations; I jumped from the bridge which crosses the Victoria Falls in central Africa. And I learned something from the experience: I discovered that I am scared of heights.

At the Falls, one of the world's top bungee operators arranges for a steady stream of tourists to throw themselves off the bridge. They even have to queue for the privilege. This queue, you might imagine, would be a good place to build up your confidence, as you watch the brave people ahead of you successfully complete the challenge. In practice, it gives you time to lose your nerve. Not least because those in front, as far as you can see, jump off the bridge and are never seen again. I discovered later that they are pulled back up and unclipped on the lower part of the bridge, out of sight of those waiting to jump.

The jumper in front of me, a young girl, was obviously terrified. Two employees helped her towards the jump point, but while her feet were edging forwards, the rest of her body was saying, 'no way'. In the end, shaking like a leaf, she chickened out and sat down to get her legs untied. Although her refusal had been recorded on video camera, she didn't appear ashamed – more relieved as far as I could see.

My sympathy for her increased as my turn got closer. All loose possessions were removed from my pockets, and a harness was tightened around my body. 'This is just for your security,' I was told, but I didn't feel greatly reassured. Then it was my turn to sit down. My ankles were tied together and the length of elastic was attached. The waiting, at least, was over, and for that I was grateful. Helpers on either side led me to the edge. Looking down, I suddenly felt real fear.

The waters of the River Zambezi were far below, one hundred metres below according to the brochure. Although I never once let go of the grab rails, my helpers encouraged me to gradually move my feet forward until I reached the edge of the metal step that stood between me and the drop. At this point, if I'd had the courage, I might have backed out. There were only 30 people watching, none of whom I was likely to see again. I could live with the disappointment – and I knew the employees weren't allowed to push me. But my rational mind talked me round. Thousands of people had done this jump and survived to tell the tale. I took a deep breath, spread out my arms and toppled forwards. *line 48*

I found myself dropping face forwards into space. Then, there was a tug on my legs, slowing me gently as I neared the river's surface. And then I was being pulled back up again – and then dropping again, and so it continued. Strangely, the fear hadn't gone when a man on a rope pulled me back towards the bridge, and what's more, it stayed with me. Not a moment too soon, I was pulled up onto the safety of solid ground. Luckily, I landed on the Zambian side of the river, where I was staying in a hotel. I was glad that I didn't have to walk across the bridge. Even though it was wide, with a high railing, I just didn't want to go anywhere near that one hundred metre drop ever again. *line 66*

1 Why hadn't the writer tried bungee-jumping before?

    A He had a fear of high places.
    B It's not possible in his home area.
    C He wanted it to be in a special place.
    D It didn't appeal to his friends.

2 According to the writer, what was the disadvantage of the queue?

    A You could see how people felt after they'd jumped.
    B It meant that other people were waiting for you to jump.
    C You could see how confident the other jumpers were.
    D It meant you had the chance to change your mind.

3 According to the writer, how did the young girl seem to feel about her experience?

    A embarrassed by her lack of courage
    B glad that the whole thing was over
    C pleased that her attempt had been filmed
    D disappointed to have wasted an opportunity

4 How did the writer feel while the equipment was being fitted?

    A relieved that his turn had come
    B impressed by the safety procedures
    C grateful for the help he was given
    D concerned about his possessions

5 What are the 'grab rails' (line 48) designed to do?

    A stop your feet slipping
    B keep you moving forwards
    C provide you with support
    D stop you looking down

6 What made the writer jump in the end?

    A It was better than being pushed.
    B He realised that he had no real choice.
    C It was better than looking silly.
    D He realised there was no great danger.

7 'it' in line 66 refers to

    A a feeling of fear
    B the bridge
    C a feeling of safety
    D the rope

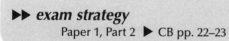
▶▶ *exam strategy*
    Paper 1, Part 2 ▶ CB pp. 22–23

▶▶ *exam tip!*
You don't need to understand every word in the text. You only need to understand in detail those parts of the text that are tested in the questions.

CLUES
Question:

1 The last sentence of Paragraph 1 tells you that A cannot be the correct answer.

2 Read the sentences 'This queue …' and 'In practice …' (paragraph 2) carefully. What does 'lose your nerve' mean?

5 What do the words 'let go' (line 47) in the text tell you about the function of the grab rails?

7 Find this word in the text. What is the subject of the sentence?

Grammar ▶ CB p.27, grammar file 14

1 Direct questions

Make direct questions by putting the words in the correct order.

1 I can where bungee-jumping go ?
   Where can I go bungee-jumping?

2 much it does cost students how for ?
   ....

3 queue there long a is ?
   ....

4 early start in how the do you morning ?
   ....

5 minimum what the age is ?
   ....

6 necessary helmet is wear a to it ?
   ....

2 Direct and indirect questions

This exercise contains both direct and indirect questions. Two of them are correct. Tick them (✓). The others contain errors. Rewrite them correctly.

1 Can you tell me where can I hire equipment?
   Can you tell me where I can hire equipment?

2 I would like to know how much does it cost a hang-gliding lesson.
   ....

3 Where I can find the instructor?
   ....

4 I need to know what to do in an emergency.
   ....

5 I would be grateful whether you could tell me what the price is.
   ....

6 Do I must wear special clothes?
   ....

7 I wonder whether I need any previous experience.
   ....

8 How many people will be there on the expedition?
   ....

3 Sentence completion

Tick the correct ending for each sentence, a) or b).

1 Could you tell ...
   a) to me where the station is?
   b) me where the station is? ✓

2 Could you explain ...
   a) the situation?
   b) me the situation?

3 I would be grateful if you ...
   a) can send me an application form.
   b) could send me an application form.

4 I'd like to know ...
   a) where I can find the information.
   b) where can I find the information.

5 Could you let me know ...
   a) when the programme starts?
   b) when does it start the programme?

4 Transformations HW

Complete the second sentence so that it has a similar meaning to the first sentence, using the word given. Do not change the word given. You must use between two and five words, including the word given.

1 Will you please send me further details? **grateful**
   I would *be grateful if you could* send me further details.

2 When should I arrive? **tell**
   Could you tell me when I should arrive?

3 Do I need insurance? **wonder**
   I wonder if I need insurance.

4 Is there cheap transport from the airport? **know**
   I would like to know about any cheap transport from the airport.

5 Will I get a certificate at the end of the course? **if**
   I would be interested to know if I get a certificate at the end of the course.

6 Do you have any places left on the camping trip? **ask**
   I am writing to ask you about any places left on the camping trip.

7 Would it be possible to leave a day early? **ask**
   I am ringing to ask it would be possible to leave a day early.

8 When do I have to pay for the course? **let**
   Could you let me when I have to pay for the course?

9 How do I get a refund for the trip that was cancelled? **tell**
   Please tell me how can I get a refund for the trip that was cancelled.

Writing: *transactional letter* ▶ CB pp.26–27

1 **1** Read the exam task opposite. Answer the questions below.

1 Who will read your letter?
　a) the editor of the newspaper
　b) the readers of the newspaper
　c) the organiser of the trip
2 Should the style be
　a) formal?
　b) informal?
　c) neutral?

2 Underline the key points in the task, then complete the following list of points to include in your letter.

a) say I'm interested
b) ....
c) ask about the conditions
d) ask about dates of trip
e) ....
f) ask about accommodation
g) ....
h) ....

2 Fill in the numbered gaps to complete the paragraph plan for your letter below.

You have seen an advertisement in a local paper asking for someone to join a group going on a trip to the Himalayas. You have decided to write for more information.

Read the advertisement and the notes you have made beside it. Then write a letter to Jean Blake to say you are interested and ask for more information.

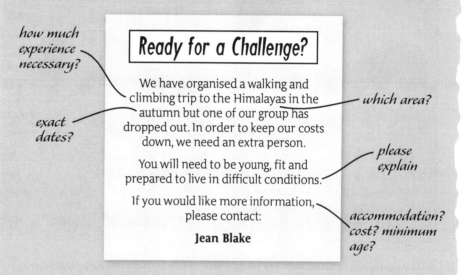

Write a letter of between 120 and 180 words in an appropriate style. Do not write any postal addresses.

Dear .... ,

Para 1: say why I am writing
(1) ....

Para 2: questions to see if I am suitable
– ask about dates
– ask about minimum age
(2) ....

Para 3: more general information about the trip
– area the trip will visit
(3) ....
– what the conditions will be like
(4) ....

Para 4: conclusion
(5) I look forward to ....
(6) Yours .... ,

3 Now write your letter. Remember to:

● use the correct greeting and ending for a formal letter.
● use formal style.
● include all the points from the task.

4 Check your work.

● Are the grammar and spelling correct?
● Have you used a variety of polite question forms correctly to find out the information you need?

Progress review 1 • Units 1–2

1 Present tenses

Look at the pictures. <u>Underline</u> the correct verb from the options given in *italics*.

These pictures (1) <u>appear</u>/*are appearing* to show scenes from two different films. In Picture 1, a man and a woman (2) *sit/are sitting* in a restaurant. They (3) *hold/are holding* hands and they (4) *look/are looking* as if they are in love! I (5) *think/am thinking* the film is probably a love story. In Picture 2 there's a young couple too, but they (6) *don't seem/are not seeming* to like each other very much! The woman (7) *shouts/is shouting* at the man. All the other customers (8) *turn/are turning* round to see what's happening. I (9) *imagine/am imagining* this is a scene from a thriller like a James Bond film, because there is a car in the background and the men getting out of it (10) *carry/are carrying* guns.

2 Future tenses

Read the conversation and put the verbs in brackets into the correct form.

Ben: Look at this poster. Two of the women who were on the polar expedition to Antarctica (1) *are giving* (give) a talk in the Town Hall next month!

Gina: Oh, I'd really like to hear more about that. What date (2) *are they* (they/come)? *com*

Ben: Just a minute. I (3) *I'll have* (have) a look! It doesn't say. (4) *Shall I* .... (I/phone) the Town Hall and find out?

Gina: Yes, good idea! They're not open now though, so you (5) .... (have to) ring tomorrow. Make sure you ring as soon as they (6) .... (open) or we may be too late!

Ben: Okay. Listen, Gina, what (7) .... (you/do) tonight? Paul and (8) .... (I/go) to the cinema. Would you like to come?

Gina: Sorry, Ben, I'd really like to but it's my sister's party tonight. She (9) *is getting* (get) married next month. She and her husband (10) *will live* (live) in Australia. Maybe next time?

3 Past tenses

Use the prompts to rewrite the story below. You will need to use the correct past tense (past simple, past continuous, past perfect simple or past perfect continuous), as well as to add missing articles and prepositions.

1 John / sit / park / last Sunday afternoon.
   John was sitting in the park last Sunday afternoon.

2 He / go / bed / late / night before / so he / feel / tired now.
   He has gone late to bad we is feeling

3 He / close / eyes and / relax.
   ....

4 They / play / favourite song / radio and so he / turn up / volume.
   ....

5 He / sit / like that / about ten minutes / when / he / suddenly / hear / noise.
   ....

6 He / look up. A small boy / stand / in front / him. It / look / as if / he / cry.
   ....

7 John / look round.
   ....

8 There / be / nobody else / around. The child / probably / run away / parents and / get lost.
   ....

9 He / speak / child / and / discover / he / wander / around / the park / for some time.
   ....

10 John / took / child / nearest police station / where / his parents / wait / anxiously.
   ....

4 Mixed tenses

1 Read the first part of the dialogue. <u>Underline</u> the correct answer from the options given in *italics*.

Carlo: Good morning. Could you tell me where (1) *I have to/do I have to* go for the auditions, please?

Receptionist: Yes, the drama studio is just along the corridor, on your left. What time (2) *did the producer tell you/the producer told you* to be here, when he phoned?

Carlo: (10) a.m. I'm a bit late. When I got in the taxi, I realised I (3) *forgot/had forgotten* my wallet so (4) *I'd had to/ I had to* go back home again. (5) *Did the producer arrive/Has the producer arrived* yet?

Receptionist: Yes, he (6) *just finished/has just finished* with the first candidate. You're just in time.

2 Now fill in the gaps in the second part of the dialogue by putting the verbs in brackets into the correct form.

Producer: Next, please!

Carlo: Hi! I'm Carlo.

Producer: Hello, Carlo. Come in. Now, I've got a few questions to ask you first. Can you tell me when (1) *you first became* (you/first/become) interested in acting as a career?

Carlo: Oh, that's easy. I (2) .... (want) to act since I was about 5 years old.

Producer: I see. What about your parents? How (3) .... (they/feel) about you going on the stage?

Carlo: Well, they're not sure. I'm afraid I (4) .... (not/tell) them where I was going when I (5) .... (leave) home this morning.

Producer: And what (6) .... (you/plan) to tell them when you get home?

Carlo: Well, I was wondering if (7) .... (you/be able) to ring them and talk to them? They (8) .... (never/speak) to a director before. I'm sure they would listen to you.

Producer: I see. Well, let's see how good you are first. What (10) .... (you/do) for this audition – act, sing, or dance?

Carlo: All three, actually! I (11) .... (do) part of a scene from the musical, 'Cats'.

Producer: Right! Start when you're ready!

5 Word formation

Use the correct form of the word in capitals at the end of each sentence to fill the gap.

1 Explorers like Shackleton were unbelievably .... **COURAGE**

2 They struggled through ice and snow and refused to give up, even when the situation seemed .... **HOPE**

3 The information they gathered during their expeditions caused a lot of .... **EXCITE**

4 Charles Darwin joined one .... expedition to the Galapagos islands. **FAME**

5 He brought back specimens and some wonderful .... of the wildlife he had seen. **ILLUSTRATE**   Illustrati ous .

6 Lexical cloze   HW

Read the text below and decide which answer A, B, C or D best fits each space. There is an example at the beginning (0).

0	A last	B latest	C final	D least

ADVENTURES IN THE FILM WORLD

The (0) ...B... blockbuster to hit our cinemas is an adventure film which was made (1) .... location in Spain. The (2) .... is quite simple; a teenager discovers (3) .... secret papers which show that the President is in danger. Then she disappears!

We interviewed the actress who (4) .... the part of the teenager in the film, Juliet Roberts. It (5) .... things did not always go well during the production. First, Juliet nearly missed being in the film. Apparently, a copy of the (6) .... , which the producer had sent her to read, got lost in the post. Then, in the middle of filming, part of the background (7) .... fell on a member of the camera (8) .... Luckily, the man was not seriously hurt but they had to (9) .... another cameraman to take his place at short notice. Something even worse happened a few days later when the director slipped and broke his leg. It (10) .... him quite a long time to recover from the shock and he had to direct the final scenes of the film from his wheelchair.

1	A on	B in	C at	D to
2	A plot	B intrigue	C drama	D line
3	A any	B the	C some	D few
4	A does	B plays	C makes	D holds
5	A looks	B seems	C strikes	D tells
6	A lines	B words	C script	D title
7	A setting	B scenery	C scene	D view
8	A party	B workers	C artists	D crew
9	A rent	B buy	C hire	D purchase
10	A needed	B used	C lasted	D took

3 Education

Vocabulary ▶ CB Reading 1 pp.28–29

1 Word formation

Use the correct form of the word in capitals at the end of each sentence to fill the gap.

1 Julia is only 15 but she has been offered a job by a top modelling .... **AGENT** *agency*
2 She has also received an .... to work in Australia. **INVITE**
3 She thinks the work would be .... exciting. **UNBELIEVABLE** *unbelievably*
4 However, her big .... is to work in the same field as her father. **AMBITIOUS**
5 Her father is an expert on .... design. **ARCHITECTURE**
6 Laura hopes to .... in Architecture at university. **SPECIAL** *specialise*
7 She wants to get some good .... before she leaves school. **QUALIFY**
8 She is studying Design and .... at the moment. **TECHNICAL**

2 Adjective/noun + noun collocations

Match a word in column A with a noun in column B to form collocations to complete the text below. Use the explanations in brackets to help you.

A	B
bright 1	4 time
late 2	break
lucky	5 scout
screen 3	1 lights
spare 4	3 test
talent 5	2 nights

Lucca Chiesa has become quite famous in the film world. His (1) *lucky break* (= *big chance*) came six months ago when he was still only 16. Lucca was spotted by a (2) ..5..... (= *someone looking for new actors*) when he was in a school play. He flew to the USA the next day for a (3) ..3..... (= *a short film test to check someone's suitability as an actor*). Then they gave him a role in a major film. The film was a great success but Lucca has decided to resist the (4) ..1..... (= *attractions*) of Hollywood for a while. He spends all his (5) ..4..... (= *hours when he is not working*) in the local film studios, but school comes first at the moment. His real ambition is to study medicine and he knows if he has too many (6) ..2..... (= *times when he doesn't get to bed early*) he will spoil his chances of going to Medical School.

Grammar and Use of English

▶ CB pp. 30–31, grammar file 10

1 -ing form or infinitive?

Underline the correct verb form from the options given in *italics*.

1 My teacher expects me *doing/to do* well in the exams.
2 Our study trip to England was fantastic! It was definitely worth *going/to go*. I really enjoyed *to see/seeing* all the places we'd read about in school. But at the end of the week, I hated *leaving/leave* all the friends I'd made.
3 I forgot to put my name on the list for swimming. Remind me *doing/to do* it tomorrow, will you?
4 Would you mind *helping/to help* me to move this desk? It's really heavy.
5 Do you fancy *coming/to come* to my house after school this evening?
6 I'm not keen on Science lessons. I don't mind *doing/to do* experiments but I hate learning formulae!
7 When my grandparents were at school, their teachers made them *to wear/wear* a uniform. Pupils were made *learn/to learn* everything by heart, too.
8 They don't let us *use/to use* the school tennis courts during the holidays, which is really annoying.

2 Change of meaning

Put the verb in brackets into the correct form.

Example:

A: Has your daughter got a role in that movie?
B: No, I regret ...*to say*... (say) (= *I'm sorry to say*) that she hasn't. In fact, I think she regrets ...*leaving*... (leave) (= *she is sorry that she left*) school now.

1 A: I'll never forget .... (dance) with you, Alicia. It's been a wonderful evening!
B: Oh, Marco! You won't forget *to phone* (phone) me tomorrow, will you?

2 **A:** Do you remember *to* .... (lock) the back door before we came out this evening?
  B: No, I don't. I hope we haven't been burgled!
  A: Oh, well. It's a good thing that I remembered .... (turn on) the burglar alarm!
3 **A:** Stop .... (drive) so fast! We've got plenty of time.
  B: Sorry! Look, I'll have to stop at this garage *to get* ..... (get) some petrol, anyway.
4 **A:** Tom and I played tennis yesterday. The match lasted for ages; in fact, we went on .... (play) until it got dark. I won the first two games but Tom went on .... (win) in the end!
5 **A:** Sorry, I didn't mean *to* .... (interrupt) you! I didn't realise you were still working.
  B: That's okay, I've nearly finished. I've got to have this project ready for tomorrow, which means .... (check) I haven't made any silly mistakes.
6 **A:** What's going on?
  B: The car's broken down. Dad's trying .... (start) it.
  A: Well, why don't we try .... (push) it? That often works.

3 Adjective + infinitive constructions

grammar file

We can use *It's* + adjective (+ of someone) + *to-infinitive* to state an opinion:
It's silly/crazy (of him) to miss school so often.

Complete the second sentence so that it means the same as the first.

1 He rang to ask how I was, which was nice.
  It was nice *of him to ring* and ask how I was.
2 She drives me to school, which is kind.
  It is kind .... me to school.
3 Jake jumped into the river to save his friend, which was brave of him.
  It was brave .... into the river to save his friend.
4 She is going to give up her job, which is foolish.
  It is foolish .... her job.
5 My friend won a prize, which was clever.
  It was clever .... a writing prize.
6 You walked home alone, which wasn't sensible.
  It wasn't sensible .... home alone.
7 Our teacher gives us a lot of homework, which is unfair.
  It is unfair .... so much homework.
8 You lost your wallet, which was careless.
  It was careless .... your wallet.

4 Verbs + prepositions

➤➤ *exam tip!*

In **Paper 3**, **Part 3**, you are often tested on your knowledge of *-ing* and infinitive forms. Remember that we always use the *-ing* form after prepositions.

Complete the sentences with a preposition from the list and the correct form of the verb in brackets. You will need to use some of the words more than once.

at / for / of / on / to

1 The headmaster congratulated me *on passing* (pass) my exams.
2 I apologise .... (not/write) to you for so long.
3 It's hard to get used .... (sit) at a desk again after such a long holiday.
4 I object *to* .... (work) while the rest of my family are lazing in the garden!
5 I'm looking forward *to meeting* (meet) your sister.
6 I'm afraid I'm not very keen *on* ...... *ing* (swim).
7 Are you good *at* .... (play) squash?
8 If you're tired .... (lie) on the beach, why don't we go shopping?

5 Transformations

Complete the second sentence so that it has a similar meaning to the first sentence, using the word given. Do not change the word given. You must use between two and five words, including the word given.

1 Many young people do not want to study beyond the age of 16. **interested**
  Many young people *are not interested in studying* beyond the age of 16.
2 It wasn't my intention to worry you. **mean**
  I .... you.
3 Their parents wouldn't allow them to go to the party. **let**
  Their parents .... to the party.
4 I don't object to studying during the holidays. **mind**
  I .... during the holidays.
5 It took us ages to get to the airport. **spent**
  We .... the airport.
6 I would prefer not to go to the concert. **rather**
  I .... to the concert.
7 I don't think you should go out tonight. **go**
  You'd better .... tonight.
8 Getting the right grades to go to university was not easy for him. **hard**
  It was *hard for him* .... the right grades to go to university.
9 Please don't let me forget to post this letter. **remind**
  Please .... this letter.

Vocabulary ▶ CB Reading 2 pp.34–35

1 Word formation

> ▶▶ *exam tip!*
>
> In **Paper 3**, **Part 5**, your knowledge of word forms will be tested. When you add items to your vocabulary book, remember to record the other forms of the word.

1 Make nouns and adjectives from each of the verbs in the table.

Verb	Noun	Adjective
1 fail	*failure* porazka	*failed*
2 employ	employment	employed
		unemployed
3 solve	solution	solved
4 occupy	occupation	occupied
5 fascinate	fascination	fascinated
6 educate	education	educated

2 Use the correct form of the word in capitals at the end of each sentence to fill the gap.

1 16-year-old Sonya Jones plans to work in advertising when she leaves school. **ADVERTISE**
2 She will have to work hard if she wants to be successful in her chosen career. **SUCCESS**
3 Unfortunately, there is a high level of unemployment this field at present. **EMPLOY**
4 Sonya's teacher is one of her strongest supporters **SUPPORT**
5 There is a strong possibility that Sonya and her family may move to Australia next year. **POSSIBLE**
6 There are far more job opportunities over there, so this could be an ideal .... to her problems. **SOLVE**

solutions

2 Prepositions and prepositional phrases

Complete the sentences below with a word from the list. You will need to use some of the words more than once.

at / by / from / for

1 My brother is very intelligent – he had learnt to read .... the age of four!
2 I'm sure I'll have a fantastic time .... university.
3 My best friend will be in Paris .... the time we finish this class!
4 I met Juan on the day I started school and .... that day on we have been the best of friends.
5 I bought Mum a cassette .... her birthday.
6 I'm sure it's not good for Chris to spend so long .... the computer.

3 Phrasal verbs

Complete the sentences below with a phrasal verb from the box. Use the definitions in *italics* to help you.

> break into   draw up   set up   settle in   work out

1 Tom has started a new school but he's finding it difficult to make friends and .... (= *feel comfortable*).
2 I can never .... (= *calculate*) the answers to mathematical equations!
3 My brother is planning to .... (= *start*) his own business next year.
4 We asked an architect to .... (= *design*) plans for our new house.
5 Our teacher caught someone trying to .... (= *enter illegally*) the school computer programs.

4 Choosing the right word

Underline **the correct word from the options given in *italics*.**

1 Irma *pursues/attends* a private school in the city centre.
2 My dad's going to *invest/generate* the money he won on the lottery in his business.
3 Natalie is ill so I suggest we *miss/postpone* the party until next week.
4 I used the computer to help me *solve/raise* a problem I had with my homework.
5 Why have you *missed/lost* so much school recently?
6 I *use/spend* a lot of time on the Internet these days.
7 My dad *insisted/persuaded* me to stay at school.
8 Tom's hobbies haven't *harmed/injured* his education.

Vocabulary and Use of English ▶ CB pp.36–37

1 Choosing the right word

Complete the sentences below with the correct word. Use each word once only.

lecturer	professor	tutor

1 I have a piano lesson at home every week with my very own private ....
2 Mr Brown has reached the very highest rank in the university and is now a .... of Surgery.
3 My neighbour has just got a full time job as .... in Economics at our local college.

pass	fail	take

4 Unless you study more, you will .... your exams.
5 I'm nervous because I'm due to .... a big exam tomorrow.
6 If I .... my driving test, Dad says he'll buy me a car!

space	room	place

7 I'm hoping to get a .... at university to study Medicine.
8 There's no more .... on the coach, I'm afraid. You'll have to wait for the next one.
9 There isn't nearly enough parking .... outside the school.

degree	licence	certificate

10 I've lost my birth .... but they've agreed to type out another one for me.
11 Julia left university with a first class .... in Biology.
12 You have to do a written and a practical test before you can get a driving ....

2 Lexical cloze

Read the text below and decide which answer A, B, C or D best fits each space. There is an example at the beginning (0).

0 **A** became **B** got **C** achieved **D** reached

A FAMOUS WRITER

Joanne Rowling **(0)** ..*A*.. famous almost overnight. She is the **(1)** ..... of a highly successful series of books for young people.

Joanne has **(2)** ..... of being a writer for as long as she can remember. In fact, she has been **(3)** ..... stories and characters ever since she was a schoolgirl. When she was still quite young, the family **(4)** ..... to a town called Chepstow. A family who lived **(5)** ..... were called Potter, and she used their name for the hero of her books. She and her sister, Di, **(6)** ..... a state school in the town. At school, she was hard-working and rather reserved. She was particularly good **(7)** ..... English and languages. Her talent for telling stories made her a popular figure in the school. During breaks between **(8)** ....., she was often surrounded by a **(9)** ..... of friends, anxious to hear the **(10)** ..... story she had written. She often included her **(11)** ..... in her stories, although they were not always aware of this!

When she left school, Joanne succeeded in getting a **(12)** ..... at university. After graduating, (she got a **(13)** ..... in French), Joanne worked as a **(14)** ..... in a school in Portugal. She married a journalist but, sadly, the couple soon **(15)** ..... and she moved to Edinburgh. She had no income and couldn't even afford a plastic folder to send her new book to potential publishers. However one wonderful day a publisher said 'yes'. It was the greatest day of her life.

	A		B		C		D	
1	**A** novelist	**B** composer	**C** author	**D** artist
2	**A** intended	**B** wanted	**C** liked	**D** dreamt
3	**A** doing up	**B** taking up	**C** putting up	**D** making up
4	**A** removed	**B** moved	**C** migrated	**D** transferred
5	**A** next	**B** near	**C** across	**D** nearby
6	**A** attended	**B** went	**C** frequented	**D** studied
7	**A** in	**B** at	**C** for	**D** on
8	**A** lectures	**B** sessions	**C** tutorials	**D** lessons
9	**A** crowd	**B** row	**C** queue	**D** procession
10	**A** last	**B** recent	**C** latest	**D** ultimate
11	**A** fellows	**B** colleagues	**C** pupils	**D** classmates
12	**A** place	**B** room	**C** seat	**D** space
13	**A** certificate	**B** diploma	**C** degree	**D** licence
14	**A** professor	**B** lecturer	**C** trainer	**D** teacher
15	**A** broke down	**B** broke out	**C** broke up	**D** broke into

Reading: *gapped text*

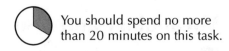

You should spend no more than 20 minutes on this task.

You are going to read a short story in which an old lady remembers her schooldays. Eight sentences have been removed from the story. Choose from the sentences **A–I** the one which best fits each gap (**1–7**). There is one extra sentence which you do not need to use. There is an example at the beginning **(0)**.

First Day at School

ONE MONDAY afternoon, Ivy was very surprised to see her daughter Anne and little granddaughter Joy. 'This is a funny time to visit me,' she said. 'Is everything all right?'

'It's Joy,' replied Anne, 'it was her first day at school today and she's refusing to go back tomorrow, but she won't tell us what happened. **0 I** '

Anne went to make some tea, leaving Ivy alone with her granddaughter. 'Tell me what happened,' prompted Ivy after a while. Joy said in a rush: 'I got the sums wrong, then I upset the paint, then I broke a boy's ruler and so he chased me. **1** She was horrid. I'm not going back! Tell me a story, please Grandma.'

Ivy smiled. 'I'll tell you about my first day at school – but if it sounds worse than yours, then you'll have to go to school tomorrow. Is it a bargain?'

Joy nodded her head.

'All right, then,' said Ivy. 'When I was your age, girls had to wear a white pinafore over a blue dress.'

'What's a pinafore?' asked Joy.

'It's a sort of white apron with pockets.'

'What a funny thing to wear to school!'

' **2** Anyway, I didn't know any of the other children, so I felt a bit lonely on my first day. The teacher looked very serious and, when she suddenly called out my name, I was terrified! **3** She said: "Ivy Wilson, you cannot come to school with hair like that. You must tie it back!"'

"Please miss, I haven't got a ribbon," I answered in a whisper. So she gave me an old piece of string. All the other girls with long hair were wearing ribbons, so I felt ridiculous.'

'Poor Grandma!' said Joy sympathetically.

'Everything seemed to go wrong after that,' continued Ivy. 'In the break, we had to go outside and do skipping. I tried my best, but for some reason I got out of step with everyone else. So the teacher made me stand aside and just watch the others. **4** '

'You had a horrid day but mine was just as bad!' said Joy.

'I haven't finished yet!' retorted Ivy. 'Lunchtime was worse. We had to eat in the school dining-room and you had to finish everything on your plate. **5** I was extremely hungry by this time. But then I saw they were serving the food I hated most: liver. I sat down and started to eat the vegetables, but every time I looked at the liver, I felt sick. Finally, when I thought that nobody was looking, I picked the liver up in my handkerchief and put it in my pocket!'

Joy looked at her grandmother with a new respect and asked, 'Did anyone see?'

'No, they didn't. The final lesson was reading. We took our pinafores off and sat in a circle, taking turns to read, which I was normally quite good at. **6** '

'The girl next to me, who was called Rose, read perfectly and the teacher praised her at the end. Then we all went to collect our pinafores, which were hanging up outside. To my horror, I saw a stain on my pinafore pocket where the juice from the liver had soaked through. Suddenly, the teacher shouted: "Who does this pinafore belong to?" pointing to mine. **7** But before I could reply, Rose said, "It's mine, miss – I had a nosebleed after lunch and my hankie got messy!" The teacher said: "Oh really? Well, make sure it's clean for tomorrow!" After that, Rose was my best friend. So, Joy, was my day worse than yours?'

'It certainly was – so I'll go back to school tomorrow,' replied Joy with a sigh.

A   I didn't expect this to be a problem, though.

B   I walked slowly to the front of the classroom and looked up at her.

C   I fell over and the teacher told us both off.

D   I thought exactly the same thing, but it was the rule.

E   I thought I was going to get into real trouble this time.

F   I was so nervous about what I'd done, however, that I kept making mistakes.

G   I felt that it hadn't really been my fault.

H   I felt so disappointed with my efforts.

I   I thought you might be able to find out.

▶▶ *exam strategy*
Paper 1, Part 3 ▶ CB p.34

▶▶ *exam tip!*
Read the whole text before you look at the extracts. Then look for reference links between the extracts and the sentences before and after each gap.

CLUES

Question:

1   The gap is followed by the word 'she'. Who is 'she'?

2   Before the gap Joy is expressing an opinion. Which of the options could be a response to someone giving an opinion?

3   Before the gap, the teacher called out her name. What do you think Ivy did when she heard her name? Look for a pronoun link to 'the teacher.'

4   How do you think Ivy felt?

5   In the sentence after the gap, Ivy mentions how hungry she was. Does this suggest she would have difficulty eating everything or not?

7   Why did the teacher shout? Is it the first thing that Ivy has done wrong? What will happen if the teacher discovers what she has done?

Grammar ▶ CB p.39

grammar files 18,19

Conditional linking words

- We can use **as long as**, **provided (that)**, or **on condition that** instead of **if** to show there is one major condition:
  *I'll lend you the money **as long as** / **provided (that)** / **on condition that** you pay it back tomorrow.*

- We can use **unless + present tense** instead of **if not** to talk about the future:
  ***Unless** we hurry, we'll miss the bus.* = If we don't hurry, we'll miss the bus.

- We use **in case + present simple / past simple** to give a reason for an action:
  1 *If I were you, I'd take an umbrella **in case** it rains.* (= because it might rain)
  2 *We booked our tickets in advance **in case** they sold out.*

1 Tenses in real and unlikely conditionals

<u>Underline</u> the correct tense from the options given in *italics*.

1 If there *is/will be* a school trip abroad next year, let's go!
2 We should take lots of magazines to read, in case our flight *is/will be* delayed.
3 The teacher will go mad unless you *do/don't do* your homework properly tonight.
4 If I *weren't/wouldn't be* so lazy, I would join the sports club.
5 Let's go swimming tomorrow if the sun *shines/will shine*.
6 Unless you *save/will save*, you *don't/won't* be able to afford to come to the concert.

2 Extra word

Two of the sentences below are correct. Tick them (✓). The other sentences contain one unnecessary word. Cross out the words.

1 Don't let your brothers play with this guitar in case they ~~will~~ break it.
2 Unless I will save my money, I won't be able to go on the trip.
3 If I would had more money, I could buy a motorbike.
4 I can't go to university unless I don't pass my exams.
5 If I didn't have to go to school every day, I could help my dad on the farm.
6 We can stay out late provided we do ring my parents.
7 Ring me if you will decide to go out tonight.
8 I wouldn't go to that disco if I were you.

3 Transformations

Complete the second sentence so that it has a similar meaning to the first sentence, using the words given. Do not change the word given. You must use between two and five words, including the word given.

1 I don't think you should wear that ring to school.
   were
   If I ...*were you I wouldn't*... wear that ring to school.
2 I'll go to the concert on condition that you pay for me.
   provided
   I'll go to the concert .... for me.
3 If you work hard, you will get to university.
   long
   You will get to university .... hard.
4 I'm not going on the school trip because I can't afford it.
   if
   I would go on the school trip .... it.
5 You'll miss the bus if you don't hurry up.
   unless
   You'll miss the bus .... up.
6 I can't come to the disco because it's my grandmother's birthday.
   it
   I could come to the disco if ....
   my grandmother's birthday.
7 I haven't got enough money to pay for my ticket.
   more
   If .... could pay for my ticket.
8 I don't think you should spend so much time in front of the computer.
   you
   If I .... spend so much time in front of the computer.
9 I won't go to the cinema without Paul.
   unless
   I won't go to the cinema .... too.
10 Bring a jacket to the barbecue because it might rain.
   case
   Bring a jacket to the barbecue ....

Writing: *transactional letter* ▶ CB pp.38–39

1 **1 Read the exam task opposite. Answer the questions below.**

1 Who should you write to?
  a) the school director
  b) Sam
2 Should the style be:
  a) formal?
  b) informal?

2 <u>Underline</u> the questions you need to answer in the task and then complete the list below.

a) which school?
b) number of hours a week?
c) ....
  ....
d) ....
  ....
e) ....
  ....

3 Tick the points in your list where you need to think of your own reasons.

2 **Choose one sentence or phrase from a) or b) that would be suitable for an informal letter.**

1 a) I am writing in reply to your letter of …
  b) Thanks for your letter – it was great to hear from you.
2 a) About accommodation, …
  b) With reference to accommodation, …
3 a) If you have any further questions, please do not hesitate to contact me.
  b) Let me know if you need any more information.

3 **Write your letter. Remember to:**

- plan before you write.
- organise the points logically.
- divide your letter into paragraphs.
- use informal style.

4 **Check your work.**

- Does your letter have a suitable greeting and ending?
- Is the style suitable for a letter to a friend?
- Have you included all the points?
- Have you used conditional sentences correctly?

You are on an English language course in Britain and have sent your pen friend, Sam, some information about it. Sam would like to go on a course as well but wants to ask your advice about the different choices. Read Sam's letter, the advertisement you sent him and the notes you have made. Then write a letter to Sam giving your advice.

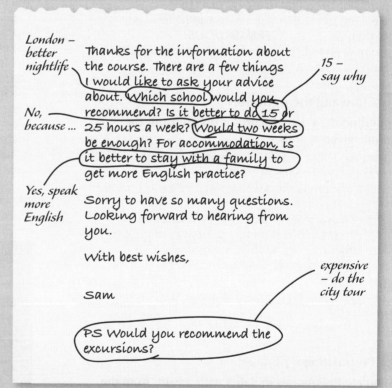

☆ **ENGLISH LANGUAGE COURSES** ☆
Come and learn English with us. We offer:
2 schools – London and Southend on Sea
Study for 15 or 25 hours a week
Lots of organised excursions
Courses 1, 2, 4 or 12 weeks
Accommodation can be arranged for you with local families or in student hostels.

London – better nightlife

Thanks for the information about the course. There are a few things I would like to ask your advice about. Which school would you recommend? Is it better to do 15 or 25 hours a week? Would two weeks be enough? For accommodation, is it better to stay with a family to get more English practice?

No, because …

15 – say why

Yes, speak more English

Sorry to have so many questions. Looking forward to hearing from you.

With best wishes,

Sam

expensive – do the city tour

PS Would you recommend the excursions?

Write a letter of between 120 and 180 words in an appropriate style. Do not write any postal addresses.

▶▶ *exam tip!*

Where you are asked to give reasons for something, you must remember to include them in your answer, otherwise you will lose marks. You will have to think of your own reasons, so make sure they suit the situation.

4 Places

Vocabulary ▶ CB Reading 1 pp.40–41

1 Word formation

Use the correct form of the word in capitals at the end of each sentence to fill the gap.

1 Life in our village is very .... **PEACE**
2 I think we are all extremely .... to live here. **FORTUNE**
3 We have a lot more .... than city kids. **FREE**
4 I find it .... that anyone wants to live in an overcrowded city. **CREDIBLE**
5 There is so much noise and .... in towns and cities. **POLLUTE**
6 My brother, however, enjoys all the .... attractions you find in a city. **CULTURE**
7 He went to London last month and he enjoyed himself .... **TREMENDOUS**
8 He may go to live in London permanently but he hasn't reached a .... yet. **DECIDE**

2 Choosing the right word

<u>Underline</u> **the correct word or phrase from the options given in** *italics.*

1 For Lisa, living in a city has benefits but it also has *drawbacks/advantages*.
2 The worst problems, *following/according* to Lisa, are noise and pollution.
3 Sometimes she *loves/longs* for the countryside.
4 Her parents live in the *suburbs/subway* of the city.
5 Her father *runs/invests* his own business.
6 She has a very good *situation/relationship* with her parents.
7 *Despite/Although* the disadvantages, she has to live in the city.
8 Prices keep *going off/going up*, so life is very expensive.

3 Prepositional phrases

Complete the phrases in italics with a word from the list.

whole / control / mess / means / budget

1 Manuel likes city life, but as a poor student, he has to manage *on a* very small ....
2 He realises that city life is *by no* .... perfect.
3 A few years ago the economy was *in a* ....
4 There was a lot of unemployment and the crime rate was *out of* ....
5 Things are much better now, *on the* ....

Grammar and Use of English

▶ **CB pp.42–43, grammar file 3**

1 Comparatives and superlatives

Fill the gaps in the sentences below using a comparative or superlative form of the word in brackets. You will need more than one word in some gaps.

1 The traffic problem in this city is much ....*better*.... than it was two years ago. (good)
2 Walking round the city at night used to be far .... than it is now. (dangerous)
3 People in my village are much .... than in the city! (friendly)
4 The bus stops here. If you want to go any ...., you'll have to take a taxi. (far)
5 That's by far the .... building I've ever seen! (ugly)
6 The longer I live in the city, the .... I feel. (happy)
7 The inhabitants of that city are the .... people in the country! There are lots of jokes about their laziness. (hard-working)
8 There are considerably .... crimes in this city than there used to be. (few)
9 I was pleased that the suburbs of the city were much .... than the centre. (polluted)
10 My city is definitely the .... place in the world! (crazy)

2 *too* and *enough*

grammar file 3

A *too*
- *too* + adjective/adverb + *to*-infinitive:
  '*I'm (far)* **too tired to go** *dancing tonight.*'
- *too* + adjective/adverb + *for* me/him/them, etc.
  + *to*-infinitive: *It was* **too late for us to go out**.

B *enough*
- *(not)* enough *(+ noun)* + *to*-infinitive:
  Tom doesn't earn **enough (money) to buy** *a car.*
- *(not)* adjective/adverb + *enough* + *to*-infinitive:
  We're **(not) hungry enough to eat** *now.*
- *(not)* adjective/adverb + *enough* + *for* me/him/
  them, etc. + *to*-infinitive:
  Our parents (don't) live **near enough for us to visit**.

1 Rearrange the words to make correct sentences.

1 the quickly much spoke too guide
  The guide spoke much too quickly.
2 I'm enough not to tired bed go to
  ....
3 that is for swim too in dangerous river people to
  ....
4 the for slow too music to dance us was to
  ....
5 make ticket enough you money pay your to sure have for
  ....
6 the too me shelf high was reach for to
  ....
7 the along drive too us were roads narrow for to
  ....
8 he me explain for enough didn't to clearly understand
  ....

2 Correct the mistakes in the sentences below.

! *too*

Do not repeat the subject after *too*.
That milk is too sour to drink. ✓
That milk is too sour to drink ~~it~~. ✗

1 The coffee was too hot to drink it.
  The coffee was too hot to drink.
2 I'm not enough strong to lift that suitcase.
  ....
3 It was raining so the bench was too wet to sit on it.
  ....
4 He was very tired to go to the party.
  ....
5 It's too late for to go out.
  ....
6 The streets aren't wide enough to drive along them.
  ....

3 Transformations

Complete the second sentence so that it has a similar meaning to the first sentence, using the word given. Do not change the word given. You must use between two and five words, including the word given.

1 The countryside is a lot less polluted than the city. **more**
  The city *is much more polluted than* the countryside.
2 As cities get bigger, they become more exciting.
  the
  The bigger cities .... they become.
3 At midday it's so hot that we can't work. **too**
  It's .... work at midday.
4 Are there any flights to Athens which are cheaper than this? **flight**
  Is this .... Athens?
5 The train is more expensive than the coach. **cheap**
  The train .... the coach.
6 I have never seen such a tall building before. **I**
  This building is the .... seen!
7 I'm too young to drive a car. **enough**
  I'm .... drive a car.
8 I can't understand them because they speak so quickly.
  me
  They speak .... understand.

4 Verb patterns

▶▶ *exam tip!*

In **Paper 3**, pay particular attention to words like *seem*, *appear*, *feel* and *look*. These verbs are used in the following ways:
- *seem/appear* + adjective:
  The people **seem** *friendly.*
- *seem/feel/look* + *like* + noun phrase:
  It **seems like** *a friendly town.*
- *seem/appear* + *to*-infinitive:
  The shops **seem to close** *early in this town.*
- *seem/feel/look as if* + clause:
  It **seems as if** *everybody has gone out.*

◀◀

Find the mistakes in these sentences and rewrite them.

1 I feel to be hungry.
  I feel hungry.
2 The disco appears like closed.
  ....
3 She looks to be a fashion model.
  ....
4 The people in this city don't seem understand English.
  ....
5 It looks to rain this afternoon.
  ....
6 Mum doesn't look like she's very pleased with us today!
  ....

5 Error correction

Read the text below and look carefully at each line. Some of
the lines are correct, and some have a word which should not be
there. If a line is correct, put a tick (✓) in the space by the number.
If a line has a word which should not be there, write the word
in the space. There are two examples at the beginning (0 and 00).

CITY LIGHTS

0	✓	I was born in a small country town. When I was young
00	as	it seemed as an ideal place to live. I had lots of friends
1	......	to play with and I was enough happy. But, as I got older,
2	......	everything suddenly seemed like a bit boring. I wanted
3	......	to go to museums and theatres but they were too far away
4	......	to get to them very often. Then, when I was 16, we moved
5	......	to London because my father was offered a much more better
6	......	job in a big hospital in the city centre. At first, my brothers
7	......	and I were very unhappy. The people in the city seemed be
8	......	really unfriendly to us. However, we made friends eventually and
9	......	we slowly realised there was a lot much more to do in the city than
10	......	in the country. Near our house, for example, there was a fantastic
11	......	amusement park. It was the most greatest place I could imagine!
12	......	We used to spend as much time as than we could there. We were
13	......	too young for to go on many of the rides, but we loved the
14	......	atmosphere. When I was a little more older, I discovered many more
15	......	exciting places to visit. The more I saw, the more than I liked London.

Vocabulary ▶ CB Reading 2 pp.46–47

1 Adjective + preposition collocations

Two of the sentences below are correct. Tick them
(✓). The other sentences contain adjectives that are
followed by the wrong preposition. <u>Underline</u> the
mistake and write the correct preposition.

1 My brother isn't very enthusiastic <u>on</u> going to the
theatre. *about*
2 Our friends are all mad in computer games.
   ....
3 I am really proud over my village. ....
4 The film was very long and we were soon bored with
   it. ....
5 I'm going to the carnival but I'm a bit worried with
   my costume. ....
6 My sister is really good in folk dancing. ....
7 I'm tired with living in a village. ....
8 I've never been very keen on foreign food. ....

2 Prepositions of place and movement

<u>Underline</u> the correct word from the options given
in *italics*.

1 My house is not far *off/from* the station.
2 When you come out *of/from* the airport, turn left.
3 Drive *on/along* the road as far as the traffic lights.
4 He lives *in/at* a very expensive area.
5 We ate our meal *on/in* the open air.
6 They arrived *in/at* London last night.
7 They strolled *on/around* the city centre.
8 He returned *to/at* Rome last night.
9 We can go out to a restaurant tonight or eat *in/at*
   home.
10 I have been *to/at* Paris twice before.

Vocabulary and Use of English

▶ **CB Reading 1 pp.48–49**

1 Word formation
Study the information in the box, then do the exercises below.

Prefixes
We use **prefixes** to form the **opposite** or **negative** of words like this:

il- + adjective	e.g. *legal – **il**legal*
im- + adjective	e.g. *perfect – **im**perfect*
ir- + adjective	e.g. *regular – **ir**regular*
in- + adjective	e.g. *dependent – **in**dependent*
un- + verb/adjective	e.g. *lock – **un**lock*
dis- + noun/verb	e.g. *belief – **dis**belief*
mis- + noun/verb	e.g. *behave – **mis**behave*

Notice that:
1 We use *il-* with many adjectives that begin with **l**.
2 We use *im-* with many adjectives that begin with **m** or **p**.
3 We use *ir-* with many adjectives that begin with **r**.

---

1 Complete the second sentence so that it has a similar meaning to the first, using the correct form of the word given.

1 That man was very rude.
That man was very *..impolite..* . **POLITE**
2 I'm afraid I don't have the same opinion as you.
I'm afraid I .... with you. **AGREE**
3 My jacket is too tight so I must open the buttons.
My jacket is too tight so I must .... it. **FASTEN**
4 Your argument does not make sense.
Your argument is .... **LOGICAL**
5 I really hate driving in the city.
I really .... driving in the city. **LIKE**
6 Her comments were not connected to the subject.
Her comments were .... to the subject. **RELEVANT**
7 I think that what you are doing is wrong.
I .... of what you are doing. **APPROVE**
8 Your parents were shocked when you left.
Your parents were shocked by your .... **APPEARANCE**

2 Three of the prefixes in the sentences below are correct. Tick them (✓). Underline the prefixes which are incorrect and write the correct word.

1 I **mistook** that boy for my brother. ......✓........
2 When the police officer saw the damage the thieves had done, he gazed at the scene with **unbelief**. ....
3 After waiting for an hour, I started getting **impatient**. ....
4 It was completely **inforgivable** of my brother to borrow your phone without asking you first. ....
5 Driving without insurance is **unlegal**. ....
6 I was **unable** to go to the carnival. ....
7 The driver nearly caused an accident because he acted completely **unresponsibly**. ....
8 The naughty children really **disbehaved** at the party. ....

2 Word formation

1 Read the text below and decide which type of word is missing from each gap (noun/verb/adjective etc.)

2 Now fill in the missing words. Use the word given in capitals below the text to form a word that fits in the space in the text. There is an example at the beginning (0).

THE STREET PARTY

The street party is a popular form of (0) ...*celebration*.... in Britain. Whole streets come together to mark such important (1) .... occasions as a new millennium. Clearly it is (2) .... to hold a party in a busy street, so traffic is banned. This may annoy motorists but it is (3) .... Street parties need the (4) .... of as many people as possible. They (5) .... people who live in cities to unite as a community just as they would in a (6) .... small village or town. Street parties are simple, (7) .... affairs, which involve a great deal of eating, drinking, dancing and general (8) .... There should be games so that small children do not get bored and (9) .... There should also be plenty of good music to (10) .... the teenagers to stay around.

---

(0) CELEBRATE	(4) INVOLVE	(8) ENJOY
(1) NATION	(5) ABLE	(9) BEHAVE
(2) POSSIBLE	(6) TRADITION	(10) COURAGE
(3) AVOID	(7) COMPLICATE	

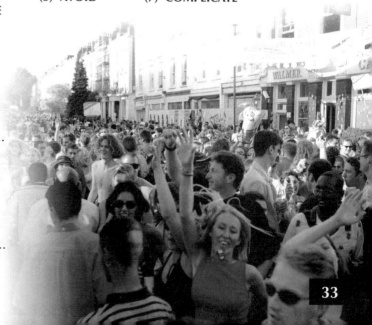

Reading: *multiple matching (questions)*

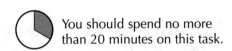

You should spend no more than 20 minutes on this task.

You are going to read a magazine article about four reporters who visited different cities. Answer the questions by choosing from the cities **A–D**. The cities may be chosen more than once. There is an example at the beginning **(0)**.

Which reporter

was fortunate with the weather conditions?	**0**	**C**
approved of an idea intended to help visitors?	**1**	
deliberately avoided one popular attraction?	**2**	
feels that a commonly-held belief is unjustified?	**3**	
followed advice about the timing of a visit?	**4**	
failed to keep to his/her original plan?	**5**	
was fulfilling a long-held intention?	**6**	
was surprised by the atmosphere in one part of the city?	**7**	
took an opportunity to make some plans?	**8**	

saw something belonging to a famous person?	**9**	
found he/she was untypical of visitors that day?	**10**	
tried something unique to the area?	**11**	
was disappointed by a well-known attraction?	**12**	
was annoyed by the behaviour of other visitors?	**13**	
mentions the source of some of his/her information?	**14**	

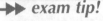 **exam strategy**   Paper 1, Part 4 ▶ CB pp.46–47

▶▶ *exam tip!*

Don't read the text word by word. Read the questions first, and underline key content words. Then scan the sections to find the answers you need. Read that part of the text carefully to make sure it matches the question.

◀◀

CLUES

Question:

5 Look for another way of saying 'plan'. Who changed his/her plan?

6 Which reporter had wanted to do something for a long time but not managed to do it until now?

11 What does 'unique' mean? Which reporter tried something new?

13 Which reporters mention other visitors? Read carefully to see which of them was annoyed.

City for a Day

We sent four reporters out to spend just a day in various world cities. Here are their reports.

A St Louis, USA

I'm just back from the USA, where I was delighted finally to visit the city of St Louis. I'd passed over it so many times high up on the interstate highway that connects more fashionable places on the east and west coasts, and I'd always promised myself I'd stop one day. In fact, although it is largely ignored by tourists, St Louis is an amazingly creative place. I had breakfast at the Blueberry Hill café, which boasts the world's finest jukebox and a guitar belonging to the legendary rock star Chuck Berry. Iced tea was invented here in 1904, but that isn't the local speciality I wanted to try. Driving out of town on the road known as Route 66, you come to Ted Drewe's famous shop which sells 441 flavours and styles of frozen custard, a sweet delicacy so popular that the police have to control the crowds at weekends. It's one US fast food that's never been franchised, so it's not available anywhere else.

B Sydney, Australia

My intention, on arrival in Sydney, had been to keep away from anything too touristy. Indeed rather than going on the classic boat tour of the harbour, I chose to have a sailing lesson there instead. As luck would have it, it was the only time I saw clouds during the whole day! When I saw the famous opera house, however, I forgot my good intentions. It was certainly worth a closer look. But after an ice-cream and the obligatory photograph, I forced myself to walk away. Almost at once I found myself in the botanical garden, which incredibly feels more like a rainforest than an urban park. Further on, I came to the legendary Harry's Café. Although famous amongst residents of Sydney as the ultimate place for a snack, I was the only customer at that moment. Harry, it turns out, is an immigrant from the north of England, as is the delicacy he serves, pie and peas.

C Cape Town, South Africa

Past experience has taught me that it's best to smile and ignore people who try to push in front of me in queues, much as it irritates me. But whoever designed the cable car that goes up Table Mountain has come up with a better solution. No sooner had I lost the race for the best viewing position at the front of the car, than the floor started to move round in a circle, so that we all got a share of the view on the way up. I'd been warned not to delay in going up the mountain. 'If you can see the top, go for it,' I was told, but I needn't have worried. By the time we reached the summit, there wasn't a cloud in sight. What's more, with the harbour and city spread out below me, it seemed the perfect place to map out the rest of my day, as I waited for the cable car to take me down again.

D London, England

I read in my guidebook that the waxwork museum Madame Tussaud's gets almost 3 million visitors a year. The Museum of London, on the other hand, only gets a tenth of that number. On the day I visited, most of the visitors seemed to be groups of young schoolchildren accompanied by their teachers, who were desperately trying to keep them together. It was quite entertaining to watch them. A frequent complaint these days is that London has too many tourists. Numbers are estimated at 26 million a year, including British tourists from other parts of the country. But the problem isn't really the number of tourists, but the fact that they all want to visit the same few attractions. For example, huge numbers go to watch the Changing of the Guard at Buckingham Palace, the Queen's official residence. Personally, I can't quite understand why this ceremony attracts any visitors at all. It takes only a few minutes, and nothing actually happens. Once it was over, I pushed through the crowds and rapidly made my escape. I had many more interesting things to see.

Grammar ▶ CB p.51

grammar file 23

A Relative pronouns

We must use a relative pronoun (*who, which, that, where, when* etc.) when it is the subject of the verb that follows. We can omit the pronoun when it is the **object**.

1 *This is the house* **which** *is haunted.* (subject)
2 *This is the house* **I live in**. (object)

B Prepositions in relative clauses

We usually put **prepositions** at the end of the clause except in formal writing.

1 *That is the hotel (that) we stayed* **in**. (informal)
2 *We visited the castle* **in which** *the King was imprisoned.* (formal)

C No preposition

We do *not* use prepositions with **where**.
That is the hotel **where** *we stayed* ~~in~~.

1 Relative clauses

Join the sentences using relative clauses. You may need to change the order of the clauses.

1 Majorca is an island. *Many people spend their holidays there.*
   Majorca is an island where many people spend their holidays.

2 There is a disco near the hotel. *It plays fantastic music.*
   ....

3 The bedroom overlooks the sea. *I share it with my brother.*
   ....

4 I've got some photographs of the house. *We stayed in it on our holidays.*
   ....

5 Our town is full of hotels. *They are empty in the winter.*
   ....

6 There is an island off the coast. *Only 50 people live there.*
   ....

7 I have just visited some friends. *Their house is near the sea.*
   ....

8 The house is absolutely huge. *My aunt lives there.*
   ....

2 Extra word

Two of the sentences below are correct. Tick them (✓). All the other sentences contain one unnecessary word. Cross out the words.

1 The man I was introduced to him was a famous architect.
2 My best friend has moved to a house which it has a huge garden.
3 That is the most beautiful city what I have ever seen.
4 My uncle bought some land which he built a beautiful house on it.
5 The hotel where the President stayed at was very expensive.
6 I loved the museum you took me to last year.
7 I think people who live in cities they are very lucky.
8 My sister lives in a village where everyone helps each other.

3 Structural cloze

Read the text below and think of the word which best fits each space. Use only one word in each space. There is an example at the beginning (0).

AN ATTRACTIVE CITY

Sydney, the city (0) .....*in*....... which I live, is the largest city in Australia. It is an exciting place, (1) .... explains why it's popular with tourists who come here. (2) .... is easy for people (3) .... live in Sidney to get to the sea. And you can find many beautiful beaches. There is Bondi Beach, for example, (4) .... you can swim or surf in spectacular waves.

There are (5) .... of parks in Sydney, which you can go (6) .... when you want peace. The city (7) .... has fantastic sporting facilities, many (8) .... which are newly-built. Sydney caters for people (9) .... interests are cultural as (10) .... as sporty. There is Sydney Opera House, which you will certainly have heard (11) ...., and many galleries and museums. There is something (12) .... everybody, whatever their interests may be.

About four million people live in Sydney, many of whom are of British descent. 1851 was an important date, because that was (13) .... gold was discovered. This is the reason (14) .... so many immigrants came to the city and settled. Newcomers are still welcome in Sydney, no matter (15) .... they are or where they come from.

Writing: *article* ▶ CB pp. 50–51

1 **Read the exam task and answer the questions below.**

> You see this notice in an international student magazine.
>
> > We are printing a series of articles about festivals around the world.
> >
> > Please send us a short article describing a festival in your country and saying what is enjoyable about it.
>
> **Write your article in 120–180 words in an appropriate style.**

1 Who will read your article?
  a) a festival organiser b) students
2 Should the style be
  a) formal? b) informal? c) neutral?
3 How many parts are there to the task?
  a) one b) two c) three

2 **1 Tick the points in the following list which you could include in your article.**

a) what people do during the festival
b) what you like about the festival
c) an occasion when something went wrong
d) what you don't like about the festival
e) preparations for the festival

2 For each point you ticked, make at least two notes of ideas that would make your article more interesting.

> *Preparations for the festival:*
> *- everyone makes special costumes*
> *- cakes are made*

3 Decide on the best order for the information. You will need at least three paragraphs. Make a paragraph plan.

3 **1 Choose the best introduction for the article in the exam task.**

a) *I think festivals are a good idea because they give people a feeling of identity with their country. They are often occasions for families to get together and enjoy themselves.*

b) *I always look forward to Bonfire night. Friends get together, light a bonfire, set off lots of fireworks and cook sausages on the fire. Sometimes the town puts on a special firework display and these can be spectacular.*

2 Choose the best conclusion.

a) *On balance, I prefer festivals that involve music and dancing. Festivals that are just eating, drinking and talking are rather boring.*

b) *Carnival time is always a good time to visit my country. You will find a wonderful atmosphere and everybody you meet will be delighted to see you.*

▶▶ exam tip!
A good introduction to an article will encourage the reader to read further.
A good conclusion will leave the reader with something to think about.

4 **Now write your article. Remember to:**
● plan before you write.
● give your article an interesting title.
● use a range of vocabulary.
● cover both parts of the task.

5 **Check your work.**
● Would the title attract the reader?
● Have you covered both parts of the task?
● Are the spelling and grammar correct?

Progress check 1

Grammar

1 Present perfect or past tenses

Underline the correct tense form from the options given in *italics*.

1 I *have never been/never went* to Brazil at carnival time.
2 I *have been doing/did* the course two years ago and I can still remember everything.
3 Sarah *has performed/has been performing* in five plays in the last three years.
4 In his first film he *played/has played* the part of a delivery boy.
5 Why *did you leave/have you left* school when you were only 16?

2 Past tenses

Put the verbs in brackets into the correct tense.

1 The family decided to emigrate because they .... (want) a better life.
2 They were exhausted by the evening because they .... (walk) all day.
3 I couldn't do the exam because I .... (not/revise) enough.
4 The explorers didn't make any progress that day because it .... (rain) all night.
5 It was the most beautiful view they .... (ever/see).
6 While I .... (study) for my exam, I only went out at weekends.

3 -ing or infinitive?

Fill each gap with the *-ing* or infinitive form of the verbs in brackets.

1 I am really looking forward to .... (go) to the carnival.
2 I must remember .... (buy) the material for my costume.
3 Michael insisted on .... (stay) until the end of the party.
4 I'm trying .... (find) a job in a theatre.
5 It's no use .... (tell) her – she won't listen.
6 It's difficult .... (study) with the television on.
7 It's not worth .... (pay) a lot of money just to see a film.
8 Can you understand all the words without .... (use) a dictionary?
9 My teacher always encourages me .... (try) new things.
10 Susanne had to move into her new house before they finished .... (decorate) it.

4 Infinitive with or without *to*?

Fill the gaps in the sentences below with a word from the list in the correct form.

make / let / allow / want

1 When I was a child, my parents refused to .... me to go rock-climbing with my friends.
2 The instructor .... us wear the proper safety helmets when we went in the cave.
3 My parents worry about me and .... me to take up safer hobbies.
4 The teacher didn't .... the students climb up the cliff.

5 Comparisons

Fill the gaps in the following sentences with the correct word.

1 The Arctic is colder .... you could ever imagine.
2 The Himalayas have some of .... most difficult climbs in the world.
3 What is the .... exciting film you have ever seen?
4 Although this actor is only a boy, he performed .... a real professional.
5 The second film wasn't nearly as good .... the first one.
6 The more frightening the film, ... more I enjoy it.
7 The play was good, but the film was even ....
8 John went to the party dressed .... a clown.
9 The cave was cold and wet. It was the .... enjoyable part of the whole weekend.
10 The .... time you spend on your homework, the better it will be.

6 Extra word

Some of the sentences below are correct. Tick them (✓). The other sentences contain one unnecessary word. Cross out the words.

1 The expedition was too much long for me to be able to do it.
2 I didn't have any clothes with me that were enough suitable.
3 This house is much too small for a family of seven.
4 It was a wonderful play and there were too many brilliant actors in it.
5 We did not have enough of food for the journey.
6 Houses in the city don't have big enough gardens.

7 Relative clauses

Join the following pairs of sentences using the relative pronoun given in brackets. Add commas where necessary.

1 Valerie teaches us French. She has just won an award. (who)
Valerie, who teaches us French, has just won an award.

2 The old lady lives at the top of the hill. Her husband was a famous explorer. (whose)
....
....

3 Do you remember that summer? We used to play by the river on the way home from school. (when)
....
....

4 I have found my own special place. I can escape from all the noise at home. (where)
....
....

5 Have you seen the latest production of Hamlet? It is on at the National Theatre. (which)
....
....

6 The book is quite cheap. I would recommend it for your revision. (that)
....
....

Vocabulary

8 Word formation
Complete the table.

	Noun	Verb	Adjective
1	origin	*originate*	....
2	....	enjoy	....
3	....	criticise	....
4	....	....	able
5	....	explain	....
6	....	equip	....
7	life	....	....
8	....	excite	....
			....

9 Word formation

Use the correct form of the word in capitals at the end of each sentence to fill the gap.

1 There was a lot of .... when the President visited the town. **EXCITE**
2 Thank you for a very .... evening. **ENJOY**
3 There was a lot of .... of the council's proposal to knock down the Town Hall. **CRITICISE**
4 I needed to think of a good .... for being late for school. **EXPLAIN**
5 Tom has an amazing .... to make people laugh. **ABLE**
6 Deep-sea diving requires a lot of expensive .... **EQUIP**

10 Prepositions

Fill the gap with the correct preposition.

1 Everybody is buying food .... preparation for the celebrations.
2 If you don't give your homework in on time, you will be .... trouble.
3 I have never been particularly good .... Maths.
4 Do you think you would be capable .... climbing at high altitudes?
5 Sam was really keen .... trying to sail around the world.
6 Our teacher has always insisted .... tidy work.
7 The same family has lived .... the house for over 200 years.
8 The view .... our balcony over the city is very beautiful.

11 Choosing the right word

Underline the correct word from each pair in *italics* in the following sentences.

1 How long does it take you to *make/do* your homework?
2 The football match attracted 10,000 *spectators/onlookers*.
3 Why don't you look *up/after* the information on the Internet?
4 Because of the bad weather, the walkers were *making/doing* very slow progress.
5 Mary was really not very *interested/interesting* in studying medicine.
6 It was the coldest night of the year and the lake was completely *freezing/frozen* over by the morning
7 It was a long journey so we set *up/out* at 4.30 a.m.
8 You will find that you learn a second foreign language much more *easily/easier* than the first.
9 I'm sure you are *capable/able* of taking the more advanced exam.
10 The highest *note/mark* you can get for the test is 20.

5 Lifestyles

Vocabulary ▶ CB Reading 1 pp.54–55

1 Word formation

Use the correct form of the word in capitals at the end of each sentence to fill the gap.

1 There is a special costume .... in our local museum. **EXHIBIT**
2 I'm going to buy some new sports .... **EQUIP**
3 I think shopping is boring, but that's just my .... opinion. **PERSON**
4 That store welcomes foreign .... wherever they come from. **VISIT**
5 Two girls at the party were very .... dressed. **SIMILAR**
6 The designer got the .... for her new dress collection from the Star Wars films. **INSPIRE**

2 Choosing the right word

Underline the correct word from the options given in *italics*.

1 I like going window shopping and seeing the *last/latest* fashions.
2 That shop *stocks/stores* a wide range of designer sports clothes.
3 This skirt is a slightly different colour from the jacket. The colours don't *match/fit*.
4 My sister wanted some *leads/tips* on how to put on her make-up.
5 In that store, you can meet famous stars and collect their *signatures/autographs* for your album.
6 I hate waiting in long *queues/crowds* in shops.

3 Prepositional phrases

Complete the phrases in *italics* with a word from the list.

stock / fact / roof / display / offer

1 They haven't got any of the trainers I wanted *in*

   ....
2 The sports clothes are *on special* .... this week so buy some while they're cheap!
3 I don't like shopping; *in* .... I find it a nightmare!
4 The clothes that are *on* .... in the shop window are not for sale.
5 In department stores you can find everything *under one* ....

Grammar and Use of English

▶ CB pp.56–57, grammar files 16,17

1 Modal verbs

Underline the correct modal verb from the options given in *italics*.

1 If I want to buy that bike I will *have to/must* save for months!
2 My parents are always telling me I *ought to/need* save my money.
3 There's a sign inside the store warning people that they *mustn't/don't have to* take any goods without paying for them first.
4 George *managed/could* to save enough from his pocket money to buy a computer!
5 I didn't know when I bought that book that you already had a copy. I *didn't need to buy/needn't have bought* it.
6 I *needn't have taken/didn't need to take* the bus into town because my father gave me a lift.
7 You *ought not/should not* to spend all your money on clothes!
8 I *need/must* buy something to wear to Jane's party.

2 Correct the mistakes

Two of the sentences below are correct. Tick them (✓). The other sentences contain mistakes with modals. Underline the mistakes and correct them.

1 Miguel is going to the shops because he needs <u>buy</u> some jeans. ...*to buy*....
2 Paul shouldn't spend all his money on himself. He's so selfish. ....
3 You needn't to wait for me. I'll catch you up later! ....
4 I must queue for 20 minutes before I could try on my new suit! ....
5 Do you have to be 18 to open an account at that store? ....
6 I'm not allowed buy any more clothes. I've got too many already! ....
7 You don't have to shoplift. If you do, you'll end up in prison! ....
8 You ought to not buy a motorbike because they're really dangerous. ....

3 Transformations

Complete the second sentence so that it has a similar meaning to the first sentence, using the word given. Do not change the word given. You must use between two and five words, including the word given.

1 We couldn't park outside the shop. **able**
   We *weren't able to* .... park outside the shop.
2 They wouldn't let us take the car for a test drive. **allowed**
   We .... the car for a test drive.
3 It wasn't necessary to pay for the goods immediately so we didn't. **need**
   We .... pay for the goods immediately so we didn't.
4 We needed three table lamps but I only succeeded in finding two. **managed**
   We needed three table lamps but I only .... two.
5 It wasn't necessary to remind her – she hadn't forgotten. **have**
   I .... her – she hadn't forgotten.

6 Soon it will be possible to buy everything over the Internet. **be**
   Soon we .... buy everything over the Internet.
7 My father told me not to waste my money. **must**
   My father told me that I .... my money
8 Jim has to wear glasses to drive. **without**
   Jim .... wearing his glasses.
9 You're not allowed to leave bicycles here. **may**
   You .... bicycles here.
10 It was necessary to go to Germany to get our new car. **to**
   We .... to Germany to get our new car.

▶▶ *exam tip!*

The error correction section of the **Use of English** paper often tests your knowledge of modal verbs. Always look carefully at the words before and after modals, to make sure that no unnecessary adverbs or participles have been added.

◀◀

4 Error correction

Read the text below and look carefully at each line. Some of the lines are correct, and some have a word which should not be there. If a line is correct, put a tick (✓) in the space by the number. If a line has a word which should not be there, write the word in the space. There are two examples at the beginning (0 and 00).

SHOPPING IN THE FUTURE

0	✓	In ten years' time, customers will be able to shop in ways that we
00	be	can't possibly be imagine now. Technology is revolutionising the
1	......	whole process of shopping. Years ago people didn't need go to the
2	......	shops every day because they could have had things delivered to
3	......	their homes. Home delivery may be quite possibly become part of
4	......	modern life, too. In fact, the process is happening already. Nowadays
5	......	we can all buy things over the Internet. We don't even have need to
6	......	leave our armchairs. I wonder if you can to imagine what an 'intelligent'
7	......	kitchen will be like in the future? It will probably contain a robot or
8	......	electronic 'housekeeper'. It may be even contain an 'intelligent'
9	......	rubbish bin. This rubbish bin may be able to manage detect when you
10	......	throw away your last tin of tomatoes. It can then 'tell' the robot
11	......	housekeeper to buy more tins of tomatoes! Soon, you won't be need
12	......	to make out a list before you go shopping. Your shopping trolley will
13	......	must be able to speak to you while you are walking round the shop.
14	......	All you will have had to do is insert your personal 'smart' card into the
15	......	handle of your trolley. The trolley will tell you what you should to buy.

Vocabulary ▶ CB Reading 2 pp.60–61

1 Word formation

Use the correct form of the word in capitals at the end of each sentence to fill the gap.

1 Tom is an interior designer and he finds his work quite .... **STRESS**
2 Kate keeps all her valuable .... under her bed. **POSSESS**
3 My friend bought a valuable ring but the things I bought were relatively .... **EXPENSIVE**
4 You can wear jeans for the dinner tonight – it will be very .... **FORMAL**
5 There were some fantastic paintings on sale in the gallery but I resisted the .... to buy one. **TEMPT**
6 I thought very .... before I decided what colour to paint my room. **CARE**

2 Choosing the right word

Underline the correct word from the options given in *italics*.

1 I've *used/spent* ages choosing furniture for my bedroom.
2 My brother leaves his things *cluttered/scattered* all over the place.
3 I *take/need* a lot of care when I buy something new.
4 As architects, my parents *lead/work* very busy lives.
5 I bought a leather sofa rather than a plastic one because I think it will *wear/last* longer.
6 Shopping always puts me in a good *atmosphere/mood*.
7 I think I *made/did* a mistake when I painted my bedroom red!
8 I hang my clothes in my bedroom *shelf/wardrobe*.
9 Do you think this scarf *goes with/suits* me?
10 I find it hard to *cope/go* with the pace of life in this city.

Vocabulary and Use of English

▶ CB pp.62–63

1 Phrasal verbs

1 Complete the sentences with a phrasal verb from the box in the correct tense.

save up	put on	show off	add up	try on	take off

1 When you've .... all the money you've spent today, you'll get a shock!
2 I'm just going to the fitting room to .... these jeans.
3 I .... all my pocket money so I could buy this computer.
4 Now I'm home, I'm just going to .... my shoes and .... my slippers.
5 I'm going to the disco tonight so that I can .... my new haircut!

2 Complete the sentences with a phrasal verb from the box in the correct tense.

throw out	work out	wear out	set out	make out

1 I've decided to .... all my old clothes and buy new ones.
2 Does this store take credit cards or will I have to .... a cheque?
3 My sister spends ages in the morning trying to .... what to wear.
4 We'll have to .... early tomorrow if we want to get to the city by 9 a.m.
5 You'll .... your new shoes if you play football in them.

▶▶ *exam tip!*

When you record phrasal verbs in your vocabulary book, try to group them in some kind of order as this will help you to memorise them. You can group them according to topic, (see Exercise 1.1 above), or according to preposition (see Exercise 1.2 above). ◀◀

2 Choosing the right word

Complete the sentences below with the correct word. Use each word once only.

trip	voyage	journey	travel

1 On our .... to America, we saw whales and dolphins from our ship.
2 I'm planning to .... to India after I leave school.
3 My dad's away on an important business .... this weekend.
4 We're going on a long .... by plane and then by jeep. We won't reach our destination for at least a week.

mean	mind	think	intend

5 What did you .... of the party?
6 Do you .... if I leave early?
7 I've never heard that word before. What does it ....?
8 What are your plans? Do you .... to open your own business eventually?

experiment	research
experience	test

9 At school today, we did an interesting science .... in the laboratory.
10 I tried surfboarding on holiday. It was a fantastic ....
11 I didn't do very well in my end of term ...., I'm afraid.
12 Scientists are doing a great deal of .... into the causes of the common cold.

3 Lexical cloze

Read the text below and decide which answer A, B, C or D best fits each space. There is an example at the beginning (0).

0 A travel **B** journey **C** trip **D** voyage

THE POWER OF PACKAGING

During a shopping (0) .C. to your supermarket, you will (1) ..... many similar products. How do manufacturers (2) ..... you to buy their products and not those of another company? By careful packaging!

(3) ..... of the boxes and bottles that you see has been carefully designed to appeal to you, personally. Do you (4) ..... about the environment? Then buy this washing powder; it contains (5) ..... chemicals. Do you want to impress your friends? Buy these trainers; they have a designer (6) ..... .

Before manufacturers market a new product, they spend months discussing the packaging. Then they (7) ..... their ideas on a group of customers. Manufacturers (8) ..... customers will see more than just a box or bottle. They want to convince you that their product (9) ..... your personality more than any (10) ..... product in the shop.

One psychologist did some interesting (11) ..... . He wanted to (12) ..... how important packaging is. He asked customers to try a certain drink. They all agreed about the taste and quality. Then he secretly (13) ..... the same drink into a differently designed bottle. The results changed! People thought this drink tasted much better than the first, (14) ..... both drinks were, in fact, the same! To the researcher's amazement, people's opinions depended (15) ..... the design of the bottle.

	A		B		C		D	
1	realise		mark		glance		notice
2	persuade		make		lead		take
3	All		Each		One		Every
4	mind		mean		care		disturb
5	fewer		less		little		much
6	badge		ticket		label		voucher
7	set out		work out		try out		carry out
8	want		wish		desire		hope
9	suits		agrees		makes		appeals
10	another		one		more		other
11	idea		study		test		research
12	make out		find out		put out		set out
13	spilt		poured		dropped		spread
14	in spite		despite		however		although
15	at		on		in		for

Reading: *multiple-choice questions*

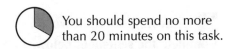

You should spend no more than 20 minutes on this task.

You are going to read a newspaper article about how to deal with unwanted possessions. For questions **1–7**, choose the answer (**A**, **B**, **C** or **D**) which you think fits best according to the text.

The Space Saver

Do you need more space in your home? Call in the expert.

William Morris, a famous English designer who was influential towards the end of the nineteenth century, once wrote: 'Have nothing in your houses that you do not know to be useful or believe to be beautiful.' A century later, thanks to the so-called consumer society, many people's homes in Britain are so jammed full of things that it is difficult for us to make good use of our available living space. If I look round my own house, for example, and apply William Morris' idea as seriously as I would like to, the task of deciding what to get rid of and what to keep seems too big to tackle alone. There are rooms you can't get into because of all the junk piled behind the door.

The answer, I have discovered, is to call in an expert. Annya Ladakh makes her living by going into people's houses and helping them to fill plastic bags with unwanted items which they then give away or sell in second-hand shops. For a consultation fee of £120, she will spend three hours helping you to assess the problem and draw up an action plan. In this way, she helps you to distinguish between your most treasured possessions and the useless 'clutter' that just seems to build up.

Most of her clients are either busy professional people who never get round to tidying up, or people setting themselves up to work from home who suddenly find they need more space. 'Often, people set off in the morning, dressed immaculately, behave extremely efficiently in their work, but return to a chaotic house,' says Annya. 'It seems strange, but they just don't *line 38* bring the work mentality home with **them**.' But what makes people want to expose their private chaos to a complete stranger, let alone take her advice? 'It can be much easier for someone outside the family to come in and give an

> *'Have nothing in your houses that you do not know to be useful or believe to be beautiful.'*

impartial view of the problem,' says Annya. 'As an outsider, I act as a fresh pair of eyes, helping them to focus on the situation.'

Sometimes, one visit will be sufficient to diagnose the problem and deal with it. But if the clutter has spread through the house and into sheds and garages, return visits may be needed to check on progress. For some clients, it might just be a matter of clearing a few shelves or installing some new ones. For others, it may mean displaying a few cherished photographs in a frame rather than keeping every one they ever took in large albums that rarely come out of the cupboard. Cuddly toys from childhood days can be the most delicate problem, regardless of the client's age, as Annya explained: 'There was one person I told recently, "Look, that panda has served you well but it has been under the bed for the last 10 years! Give it to someone who will love it."'

Generally, however, Annya finds that gentle persuasion and encouragement work better than **bullying**. *line 66* 'I point out how stressful clutter is,' she says. 'It wastes your time and can make you bad-tempered when you can't find things. Some people's social lives become affected, they are so ashamed of the mess that they stop inviting others round to their homes.'

Her experience has taught her that clutter is not just a logical question, but an emotional one, an indication, perhaps, that someone is hanging on to the past. 'It can be painful to let go of material possessions, however worthless they may be,' Annya observes. 'Especially if people have been brought up by parents who lived through a less materialistic age, when it was normal to hang onto things in case they came in handy. Nowadays, most of us simply have too many possessions.'

1 What is the writer's opinion of William Morris's idea?

   A It is not relevant today.
   B It is something she'd like to try.
   C He wanted it to be in a special place.
   D It is not to be taken seriously.

2 What service does Annya provide?

   A She helps people to make decisions.
   B She buys unwanted things from people.
   C She sells unwanted things for people.
   D She puts a value on people's possessions.

3 What surprises Annya about most of the people she works for?

   A They are too busy to be tidy.
   B They are willing to listen to her.
   C They are efficient in other ways.
   D They often bring work home with them.

4 What does 'them' in line 38 refer to?

   A Annya's eyes
   B Annya's clients
   C Annya's advice
   D Annya's views

5 Why may Annya need to see some clients more than once?

   A when she is dealing with very personal items
   B when they don't accept all of her suggestions
   C when alterations have to be made to the house
   D when there is a great deal of work to be done

6 'bullying' in line 66 means

   A wasting people's time
   B getting angry with people
   C putting people under pressure
   D making people feel embarrassed

• WILLIAM • MORRIS •

7 According to Annya, why may people not like disposing of their possessions?

   A It's a result of their upbringing.
   B They think everything they own is useful.
   C It's a result of the age we live in.
   D They think that old things may be valuable.

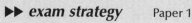 **exam strategy**   Paper 1, Part 2 ▶ CB pp.22

 **exam tip!**

Look for and underline the answers to the questions in the text <u>before</u> you read the options **A–D**. You are less likely to get confused by the options.

CLUES

Question:

1 Does the writer 'call in an expert' (paragraph 2) because she agrees with Morris or because she disagrees with him?

3 Look for a phrase in Paragraph 3 where Annya expresses surprise.

4 Find the word in the text then look back at the question that Annya has been asked.

6 Find the word in the text. Compare it with the approach that Annya uses.

Grammar

▶ CB p.65, grammar files 13, 14

1 Indirect speech

1 Complete the sentences below.

1 'I went to the shops yesterday.'
Sarah said that *she had been to the shops the day before* .

2 'Why don't you take the jacket back to the store tomorrow?'
My friend suggested that ....

3 'These jeans will be cheaper next week.'
The assistant told me that ....

4 'We're expecting new stock in later this morning.'
The manager explained that ....

5 'Will the store be open tomorrow?'
I wanted to know if ....

6 'Can I pay later or must I pay now?'
I asked the assistant whether .... or whether ....

2 Extra word

Two of the sentences below are correct. Tick them (✓). All the other sentences contain one unnecessary word. Cross out the words.

1 I asked to the assistant if I could see the manager.
2 My friend suggested me that I should try the trousers on.
3 The salesman said the jeans I had ordered would be in the shop the next day.
4 Paul explained that he had bought his coat the previous day before.
5 Sandra asked me where did I usually bought my shoes from.
6 Mrs Brown told to her daughter to save her money.
7 Sam complained that the shoes were too tight.
8 The customer insisted on he wanted his money back.

3 Transformations

Complete the second sentence so that it has a similar meaning to the first sentence, using the word given. Do not change the word given. You must use between two and five words, including the word given.

1 'The sweater shrank when I washed it,' said the customer. **complained**
The customer *complained the sweater had shrunk* when he washed it.

2 'Can I have a refund?' asked John. **whether**
John asked .... a refund.

3 'Does the shop open on Sundays?' asked John. **enquired**
John .... on Sundays.

4 'Why didn't you buy the computer?' Tina asked. **me**
Tina asked .... bought the computer.

5 'Why don't you complain, Peter?' Alan said. **suggested**
Alan .... complain.

6 'I haven't touched anything!' said Rebecca. **protested**
Rebecca .... anything.

7 'When did you buy your shoes?' the manager asked Susan. **she**
The manager asked Susan .... her shoes.

8 'I'm going to pay for the coffee,' Georgia said. **that**
Georgia insisted ....
pay for the coffee.

9 'I must buy a new computer!' Daniel said to Rachel. **to**
Daniel told Rachel .... a new computer.

10 'Would you like to try the jacket on?' the assistant asked. **I**
The assistant asked me .... to try the jacket on.

! *must* and *had to*

In indirect speech,
must becomes **had to**.
My father said I ~~must have~~
had to save my money.

Writing:
letter of correction

▶ CB pp.64–65

exam file

In **Paper 2**, **Part 1** you may be asked to write a letter in which you correct inaccurate information given e.g. in a newspaper. This will usually involve making some positive comments as well as pointing out facts that were not quite right.

1 Read the exam task on page 47 and answer the following questions.

1 Who is the letter to be written to?
   a) the editor of the newspaper
   b) the organiser of the craft fair

2 Should it be:
   a) formal?
   b) informal?

3 What is the purpose of the letter?
   a) to complain about the craft fair
   b) to point out which details in the article were wrong

2 Complete the following list of points that you have to include in your letter. Notice that some of the notes contain two parts.

a) *excellent quality goods;*
   what I bought ....
b) *too crowded – lots of tourists* ....
c) ....
d) ....
e) *delicious food; what I had* ....
f) ....
   ....

You attended a craft fair in your town and later read an article about it in your local newspaper. You enjoyed the event but feel that some details in the description of the fair are not correct. Read the article and the notes you have made beside it. Then write a letter to the editor of the newspaper giving your opinion and correcting the information using all your notes.

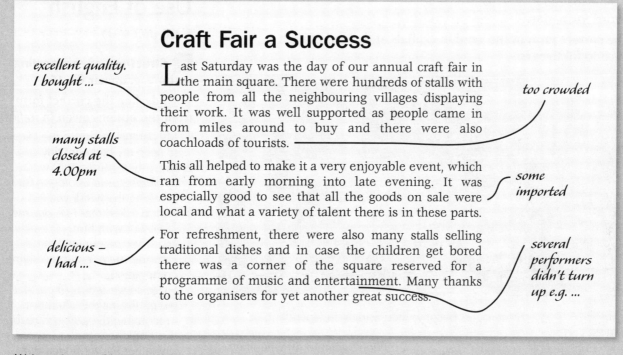

Craft Fair a Success

excellent quality. I bought ...

Last Saturday was the day of our annual craft fair in the main square. There were hundreds of stalls with people from all the neighbouring villages displaying their work. It was well supported as people came in from miles around to buy and there were also coachloads of tourists.

too crowded

many stalls closed at 4.00pm

This all helped to make it a very enjoyable event, which ran from early morning into late evening. It was especially good to see that all the goods on sale were local and what a variety of talent there is in these parts.

some imported

delicious – I had ...

For refreshment, there were also many stalls selling traditional dishes and in case the children get bored there was a corner of the square reserved for a programme of music and entertainment. Many thanks to the organisers for yet another great success.

several performers didn't turn up e.g. ...

Write a letter of between 120–180 words in an appropriate style. Do not write any postal addresses.

3 Use your points in Exercise 2 to fill the numbered gaps in the paragraph plan below. Add the extra details required.

Para. 1: *refer to newspaper article; say why I am writing*

Para. 2: *give the positive points*
   The quality of the goods was excellent. (1) ....
   ...
   The food was delicious. (2) ....

Para. 3: *give the negative points*
   It was too crowded.
   (3) ....
   (4) ....
   (5) ....

Para. 4: *What I would like to happen at next year's fair.*

▶▶ *exam tip!*

You will usually need to reorganise the order in which the points are given. You will be given credit for thoughtful organisation.

◀◀

4 Now write your letter. Use expressions like these to introduce your points:

I would like to point out ...

It is true that ... However ...

Your article said that ... but in fact ...

5 Check your work.
- Are the style and tone appropriate?
- Have you used a suitable greeting and ending?
- Are the grammar and spelling correct?

6 Family life

Vocabulary ▶ CB Reading 1 pp.66–67

1 Word formation

Use the correct form of the word in capitals at the end of each sentence to fill the gap.

1 During ...., teenagers become increasingly independent. **ADOLESCENT**
2 Some young people are rather .... and don't want to do what their parents tell them to do. **REBEL**
3 Parents should respect a teenager's need for .... **PRIVATE**
4 Teenagers get .... angry if their parents question them about things they consider private. **TERRIBLE**
5 Some young people have problems which cause them a lot of .... **ANXIOUS**
6 Parents and teenagers need to listen to each other, and to treat each other with a great deal of .... **PATIENT**
7 Some parents never let children make their own decisions and, ..., this leads to conflict. **FORTUNATE**
8 Parents and teenagers can avoid unpleasant .... if they respect each other's point of view. **ARGUE**

2 Prepositional phrases

Underline the correct preposition from the options given in *italics*. The whole phrase is in *italics* to help you.

1 Some people say teenagers are difficult but *on/in my experience* most of them are very well-adjusted.
2 Tom had a lot of problems last year and *in/at the time* his parents were really worried about him.
3 I know you feel strongly on this topic, but please look at things *from/in my point of view*.
4 I must tidy my bedroom; it's *on/in a terrible mess*.
5 Psychologists say that *on/in no account* should parents invade a teenager's personal space.
6 I know you're angry with your parents but I think more understanding is needed *at/on both sides*.

Grammar and Use of English

▶ CB pp.68–69

1 Structures after reporting verbs ▶ grammar file 15

1 Underline the correct form from the options given in *italics*.

1 My parents reminded me *I keep/ to keep* my bedroom tidy.
2 My father insisted *that we apologise/us to apologise* for breaking the window.
3 Marco asked *that I go out/me to go out* with him.
4 My sister encouraged *me entering/me to enter* the skiing competition.
5 Hugo suggested *us to go/that we go* fishing this afternoon.
6 I recommend *reading/to read* this book.
7 My father has forbidden *that I go/me to go* to the disco.
8 My friend begged me *to not tell/not to tell* her parents what had happened.

2 Tick (✓) the correct sentence in each pair.

1 A Mum said us to make our beds.
  B Mum told us to make our beds.
2 A My brother said he was leaving home.
  B My brother said me he was leaving home.
3 A My best friend told that he had a new girlfriend.
  B My best friend told me that he had a new girlfriend.
4 A She said me 'Hello'.
  B She said 'Hello' to me.
5 A I said I couldn't go to the party.
  B I told I couldn't go to the party.

2 Transformations

Complete the second sentence so that it has a similar meaning to the first sentence, using the word given. Do not change the word given. You must use between two and five words, including the word given.

1 'I wouldn't leave your wallet on the table if I were you, Franco,' I said. **to**
   I advised *Franco not to leave his* wallet on the table.

2 'I did not break your watch, Jane,' Nadia protested. **denied**
   Nadia .... Jane's watch.

3 'Why don't you phone your parents, George?' Alan said. **suggested**
   Alan .... parents.

4 'Oh no! I forgot to go to the bank this morning,' said John. **realised**
   John .... to go to the bank that morning.

5 'Be home by 11 p.m., Lisa!' her dad said. **told**
   Lisa's dad .... home by 11 p.m.

6 'Remember to buy a present for your mum's birthday, Stella,' James said. **reminded**
   James .... a present for her mum's birthday.

7 'Shall we go to the cinema?' David said. **suggested**
   David .... the cinema.

8 'I'm sorry I lost your book, James,' said Tom. **apologised**
   Tom .... James's book.

9 'I broke the window,' Perla said. **admitted**
   Perla .... the window.

10 'I'll give you a lift to the party if you like, Paul!' **offered**
   Harry .... a lift to the party.

3 Phrasal verbs

grammar file

There are four main types of **phrasal verbs**.

- **Type 1: verb + adverb** (no object)
  Prices are going up.

- **Type 2: verb + object + adverb/verb + adverb + object**
  I looked the word up earlier./I looked up the word earlier.
  Note: When the object is a pronoun, it must go between the verb and the adverb:
  I looked it up earlier.

- **Type 3: verb + preposition + object**
  I take after my father.

- **Type 4: verb + adverb + preposition + object**
  We've run out of coffee.

For Exercises 3.1–3.3, complete the sentences with a phrasal verb from the box in the correct tense.

1 These are all Type 1 phrasal verbs.

grow up   show off   lie down   break down   ~~set off~~

1 We'll have to ...*set off*.... early tomorrow morning.
2 My little brother wants to be a doctor when he ....
3 Oh, no! The car has .... again!
4 That boy came first in the exam and he's been .... ever since!
5 I don't feel well; I think I'll ....

2 These are all Type 2 phrasal verbs.

bring up   back up   pick up   let down   tell off

1 Christopher promised to come to the disco with me but he .... me .... at the last minute.
2 If I complain to the waiter that the pizzas are cold, will you come with me and .... me ....?
3 Mum .... me .... for coming home late last night.
4 My parents were working abroad when I was a child so my grandparents .... me ....
5 My dad's driving me to the party. Shall we .... you ....?

3 These are all Type 4 phrasal verbs.

run out of   put up with   go out with   go on at get on with

1 My sister is .... a rock star. They've been seeing each other for some months now.
2 I've .... patience with my brother; I'm not going to play with him any more.
3 My parents say they aren't prepared to .... my moods any longer!
4 Lucas doesn't .... his sisters, you know. They're always fighting!
5 Mum's been .... me all morning to tidy my room – she says it's disgusting!

▶▶ *exam tip!*

Always record the complete form of phrasal verbs in your vocabulary book, together with an example sentence. E.g.:
to tell someone off = to scold someone.
My teacher tells me off for the smallest mistakes!

4 Error correction

Read the text below and look carefully at each line. Some of the lines are correct, and some have a word which should not be there. If a line is correct, put a tick (✓) in the space by the number. If a line has a word which should not be there, write the word in the space. There are two examples at the beginning (0 and 00).

➤➤ *exam tip!*

In **Paper 3**, **Part 4** (error correction) you are often tested on your knowledge of prepositions and/or phrasal verbs. Typical errors are:
- **unnecessary prepositions after normal verbs**: *My dad grows ~~up~~ tomatoes.*
- **unnecessary extra particles/prepositions after phrasal verbs**: *I look ~~up~~ after my younger sister.*
- **an unnecessary object**:
  a) between a phrasal verb and the preposition/particle: *I've given ~~it~~ up learning the guitar.*
  b) after the complete phrasal verb: *My sister is always showing off ~~it~~.*
◀◀

A TIDY HOME

0	...*by*	There were eight of us in my family. We lived by in a very
00	...✓	small house. It was always untidy because we left our toys
1	......	lying down around. At first our parents picked our things up
2	......	of for us. But eventually they decided not to put up with
3	......	our untidiness any longer. They worked up out an original way
4	......	to make us tidier. They placed one big box by on the front door
5	......	for all the things that we dropped by on our way into the house
6	......	from the garden. Each of us had our own personal box indoors,
7	......	too. So, when anyone tidied the house, they could put by things
8	......	into boxes instead of taking them upstairs. Our parents made
9	......	us pay a fine if we didn't pick up to our things. We hated this
10	......	punishment more than being told it off. We didn't get much pocket
11	......	money and didn't want to waste it up on fines. So, we sat down
12	......	and worked out a schedule for tidying the house. We took off
13	......	turns cleaning and made out sure the house was tidy when our
14	......	parents came home. We have all grown it up and left home now
15	......	but we agree that our parents definitely had the right idea.

Vocabulary ▶ CB Reading 2 pp.72–73

1 Word formation

Use the correct form of the word in capitals at the end of each sentence to fill the gap.

1 When I was a child I wanted to be an .... **EXPLORE**
2 I thought it would be much too .... to stay at home and do a normal job. **BORE**
3 My mother says that I was .... adventurous when I was small. **INCREDIBLE**
4 As I got older, I began to think about .... as a career. **ACT**
5 The biggest problem about being an actor is that, unfortunately, you may face periods of .... **EMPLOY**
6 In the end, I became a theatre designer, and I am very .... of my chosen career. **PRIDE**
7 My brother is a highly .... producer. **SUCCESS**
8 My parents always support me when I have problems at work and I find that very .... **COMFORT**

2 Prepositions and prepositional phrases

Underline the correct preposition from the options given in *italics*.

1 I was amazed to see my sister *on/at the centre* of so much attention.
2 I first saw my favourite actor *on/at stage* when I was five.
3 I am *under/with no illusions* about my talents; I know I can't act!
4 I saw you *in/on television* last night!
5 My brother is going to *star in/at a new TV series*.
6 The murderer kills his victim *on/in the first scene* of the play.
7 I don't usually get frightened when I watch thrillers but *at/in the end* of that film I was terrified!
8 I knew I wanted to be an actor *since/from a very young age*.

Vocabulary and Use of English ▶ CB pp.74–75

1 Verb + noun collocations

Match the sentence halves to make logical sentences.

1 We discussed	a) three languages
2 He told	b) complete rubbish
3 She said	c) me good advice
4 She talked	d) a lie
5 They gave	e) goodbye
6 He spoke	f) the problem

2 Choosing the right word

Complete the sentences below with the correct word or phrase. Use each word or phrase once only.

while   as   during

1 .... I get on well with my parents, we do argue sometimes.
2 .... teenagers get older, they need more privacy.
3 I made a new friend .... the holidays.

as   so   if

4 I'm not sure .... I want to be an actor.
5 I want to be an interpreter, ... I'll study languages at university.
6 My friend is going to study law .... he wants to become a judge.

Although   In spite   Despite

7 Parents can't always be perfect. .... all their efforts, they often forget how hard growing up can be.
8 .... my parents try hard, they don't really understand me.
9 .... of all the unkind things he said to me last night, I still love my brother.

otherwise   even   even though

10 My brother is really bad-tempered at the moment and .... my parents are afraid to speak to him.
11 You'd better not go in Henry's room, ... he'll go really mad!
12 I love my sister .... she can be really horrible to me at times.

3 Lexical cloze

Read the text below and decide which answer A, B, C or D best fits each space. There is an example at the beginning (0).

0 **A** far   **B** great   **C** much   **D** lot

BEING A TEENAGER

Today's teenagers have **0)** ..A.. more money and expensive possessions **(1)** ..... their parents ever did. Articles like radios and bicycles, that cost a fortune **(2)** ..... decades ago, are now mass-produced and cheap. And items that nobody even **(3)** ..... of possessing a few years ago, such as mobile phones and computers, are now commonplace. Teenagers are definitely better off financially. **(4)** ..... , life is not easy for them. **(5)** ..... is much more to worry about than there was in the past. Jobs are not as secure **(6)** ..... they used to be, and teenagers can no **(7)** ..... be confident that the world will always be peaceful and free of pollution.

Teenagers drive their parents crazy **(8)** ..... many ways. Some of them spray their hair with amazing colours, **(9)** ..... others wear clothes that shock their parents. They all want **(10)** ..... own stereos, mobile phones and televisions. **(11)** ..... these young people are not really behaving differently from how their parents behaved when they were young. Many of today's parents and grandparents will laugh when they **(12)** ..... the crazy fashions they wore. Those adults, **(13)** ..... are parents now, fought with their own parents about clothes and lifestyles. **(14)** ..... , teenagers have fought with their parents **(15)** ..... time began – and no doubt they always will!

1	**A** as	**B** even	**C** than	**D** that
2	**A** a little	**B** little	**C** few	**D** a few
3	**A** imagined	**B** dreamt	**C** pictured	**D** considered
4	**A** Despite	**B** However	**C** In spite	**D** Even though
5	**A** It	**B** They	**C** There	**D** This
6	**A** like	**B** as	**C** but	**D** when
7	**A** more	**B** farther	**C** sooner	**D** longer
8	**A** in	**B** on	**C** at	**D** by
9	**A** when	**B** as	**C** meanwhile	**D** while
10	**A** an	**B** his	**C** ones	**D** their
11	**A** And	**B** Although	**C** Also	**D** But
12	**A** remind	**B** think	**C** remember	**D** review
13	**A** which	**B** they	**C** such	**D** who
14	**A** As well	**B** In fact	**C** At last	**D** At once
15	**A** since	**B** from	**C** when	**D** as

Reading: *multiple matching (questions)*

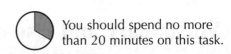 You should spend no more than 20 minutes on this task.

You are going to read a magazine article about childhood experiences. Answer the questions by choosing from the people **A–D**. The people may be chosen more than once. There is an example at the beginning **(0)**.

Which person mentions

being particularly close to a family member?

| 0 | **C** |

his/her intention to act differently from a parent?

| 1 | |

enjoying the fact that something was difficult?

| 2 | |

a way of making sure that he/she did not leave anything out?

| 3 | |

an act of great generosity?

| 4 | |

an opportunity to be creative?

| 5 | |

getting in touch with people who could be of help?

| 6 | |

regret at what may have been missed?

| 7 | |

someone who found something puzzling?

| 8 | |

someone else making a decision with his/her wellbeing in mind?

| 9 | |

learning to be more independent?

| 10 | |

purchasing something which changed his/her life?

| 11 | |

someone who is unpredictable by nature?

| 12 | |

something which is no longer available?

| 13 | |

something that was in short supply?

| 14 | |

▶▶ *exam strategy*
Paper 1, Part 4 ▶ CB p.46–47

▶▶ *exam tip!*

Look for words and expressions in the text that express the same ideas as the questions.

CLUES

Question:

2 Look for ways of indicating that the writer 'enjoyed himself/herself' and found something 'difficult'.

3 What ways can you think of to make sure you don't forget anything? Can you find one of these in the text?

7 Look at the end of each passage. Which person is looking back with regret?

10 Look for an idiomatic expression that means 'doing things on your own, without help'.

11 Look through the texts to find people who purchased things. Read carefully to find whose life changed as a result.

12 Look for a description of someone who is always doing things unexpectedly.

14 Look for an expression which means 'there wasn't much of something'.

Childhood Memories

Four successful people look back at significant events in their childhood

A COLIN

When I was eleven years old, my dad inherited quite a large amount of money from a distant relative. It was typical of him that he decided to use the money to take a whole party of local kids to Disneyland in Florida for three days. Fortunately, I was able to go as well, which was tremendous. In those days, you had to buy tickets for each ride and so we made a checklist of them all and ticked them off one by one until we'd been on every one. They still had a donkey train and a canoe ride back then. My friend Eric bought a funny hat with his name on the front and then kept wondering how, all over Disneyland, random people knew his name and kept saying, 'Hi Eric!' My family will never let me forget how I ordered a bowl of potato chips on room service at the motel, which cost them a staggering $20. They were good chips, though!

B MARILYN

Most teenagers' parents have normal jobs, you know like working in an office or being part of a company, but not my mum. She lives for her work and makes spur-of-the-moment decisions. When I was a teenager, it almost felt as if I was the parent and she was the child, as I tried to talk her out of whatever her latest scheme involved. You see, my mum's an archaeologist. She travels round the world finding exciting things in old ruins, and because she was always on the move, so was I! Sometimes I used to wonder if we'd ever settle down and lead a normal family life, but we never did, which is a shame really. Of course, now I'm going to make sure that I don't do the same to my daughter.

C JEREMY

I suppose being twins, my brother and I were always regarded as a single unit and we did do everything together. From an early age, we were into inventing things, especially things which exploded like rockets, although I don't ever recall any actually leaving the ground. We were keen on Maths at school and bought a computer when we were eleven years old. It was the best time for getting into computers because there was very little software about in those days, so if you wanted to make the computer do anything, you had to write it yourself. Before long we were selling the stuff we'd written to software companies. I don't think we knew how to turn our interest into money at that stage, having no commercial experience. But we soon found plenty of people who did know, but who couldn't handle the technical side. We haven't looked back since.

D TANYA

When I was a teenager, my parents used to send my brother and me off on a week-long summer activity camp each year. Actually, we went to the same place five years running. I think it was because they wanted us to do something outdoors rather than have us sitting in front of a computer screen at home. And it was certainly challenging, if you consider we learnt to do things like climbing and caving. It wouldn't suit all kids, but for us it was great. We found out how to fend for ourselves and we met lots of people from around the world. I'm still in touch with some of them by e-mail even now. Looking back, I guess it cost my parents a lot of money, but as far as I'm concerned it was a good investment because it really broadened my horizons.

Grammar ▶ CB p.77, grammar file 7

1 used to and would

! Position of adverbs

We put adverbs of frequency in front of **used to** but after **would**.

1 *I **always** used to like sweets as a child.*
2 *I didn't **always** use to behave well in class.*
3 *I would **never** play with my sister.*

<u>Underline</u> the correct option from those given in *italics*.

1 I can't *get/be* used to living next to a pop star!
2 We used to *live/living* near the sea when we were children.
3 I am getting *use/used* to being on my own.
4 Sandra *would/used to* be frightened of the dark.
5 I didn't *use/used* to play tennis regularly but I do now.
6 My brothers and sisters *always used to/always would* tease me when we were young.
7 Has he *been/got* used to living with his grandparents now?
8 Did you *use/used* to fight with your brothers and sisters?

2 used to or get/be used to?

Match the sentence halves to make logical sentences.

1 Did you
2 Are you
3 I'll never
4 In the past, Linda always
5 Miguel
6 Sarah can't get

a) used to argue with her brother.
b) get used to living in this town.
c) used to working abroad.
d) use to share a room with your sister?
e) used to live with his grandmother.
f) getting used to speaking English?

3 Structural cloze

Read the text below and think of the word which best fits each space. Use only one word in each space. There is an example at the beginning (0).

GROWING UP

How much do you remember about your early childhood? (0) ....*Did*...... you use to be a little devil or were you the teacher's pet? My dad used to (1) .... really wild, but of course he doesn't like to admit it now!

As a child, my father used (2) .... live on a farm. Every day, he and his friends (3) .... go and play in the fields. They (4) .... quite used to (5) .... on their own, and never wanted any adults to entertain them. They would swim in the river and (6) .... their bikes along the country lanes. They (7) .... used to come home until late and were always getting into trouble.

Then my father started school. It was really difficult for him to (8) .... used to studying all day! He just couldn't get used to (9) .... on a chair for hours and listening to the teacher. The teacher would (10) .... at him loudly but it was no good. Luckily, when he got home my grandparents were always busy on the farm and they rarely (11) .... to ask him about school. However, his teacher (12) .... getting more and more irritated with him. 'I (13) .... not used to having such disobedient children in my class!' she would cry. 'If you haven't (14) .... used to this classroom by now, you never (15) .... ! I shall write to your parents.'

Writing: *story* ▶ CB pp.76–77

1 1 Read the exam task.

You have been invited to write a short story for a competition. The story must begin with these words:

> *As she rang the doorbell, Susan felt a mixture of fear and excitement.*

Write a story of 120–180 words.

2 Answer the following questions with your own ideas to help you plan your story. Write notes.

1 Who is Susan?

....

2 How old is she?

....

3 Whose door was she standing at?

....

4 Why did she feel fear and excitement?

....

5 What had happened before?

....

6 What happened after she rang the doorbell?

....

7 How did the story end?

....

2 1 Look at these paragraph topics for a story and number them in the most logical order to make a paragraph plan.

☐ a) the result of the main event

☐ b) introduce the main character

☐ c) the main event

☐ d) the background to the story (setting the scene)

2 Match each question in Exercise 1.2 with one of the paragraph topics in Exercise 2.1.

Example: 1 b)

3 Choose the best opening paragraph.

1

As she rang the doorbell, Susan felt a mixture of fear and excitement. She had only lived in the area for a few weeks and she was not sure what to expect from this particular house. She had had a letter inviting her to go there and find out something she had always wanted to know.

2

As she rang the doorbell, Susan felt a mixture of fear and excitement. Susan got up in the morning and went to school as usual. It wasn't until later in the day that she realised she had forgotten to go to get her examination results from her teacher's house.

3

As she rang the doorbell, Susan felt a mixture of fear and excitement. I had always been afraid of things I didn't know about and this occasion was particularly bad because I had heard so many strange stories about the house on the hill.

4 Now write your story. Remember to:

- start your story with the given sentence.
- write in the past tense.
- give your story a title.

▶▶ *exam tip!*

It is very important that your story follows on from the first sentence. Be careful not to jump to another time or place and don't change the main character. ◀◀

5 Check your work.

- Does the story follow on logically from the given sentence?
- Is it divided into paragraphs?
- Have you used a good range of vocabulary and structures?
- Is the language correct?

Progress review 2 • Units 3-6

1 -ing forms and infinitives

Read the conversation and put the verbs in brackets into the correct form, -ing or infinitive.

A: Well, it's our last day at school, Anna. How do you feel about (1) ..*leaving*.... (leave)?

B: I don't know really. I'm looking forward to (2) .... (go) to university, but I hate (3) .... (have to) say goodbye to all my friends here.

A: I know. Do you remember our first day at school? You kept trying (4) .... (escape) by climbing through the windows. In the end, the teacher had to lock all the doors and windows!

B: I know. I really didn't want (5) .... (go) to school in the beginning. I used to beg my mum to let me (6) .... (stay) at home with her. I tried (7) .... (tell) her all sorts of nonsense – like I was ill, or that the teachers were horrible to me – but that never worked! In the end, I realised that it was no good (8) .... (fight) about it – I'd just have to put up with (9) .... (go) to school.

A: Well, I'm glad we were in the same class. Do you remember the time I jumped into the deep end of the swimming pool by mistake and I thought I was drowning? You heard me (10) .... (shout) for help and jumped in too. You held my head up and stopped me from (11) .... (go) under. After that, we went to the pool every evening and you taught me (12) .... (swim) properly.

B: Yes, we've had some good times together. Never mind, we'll still keep in touch, won't we?

A: Of course we will!

2 Real and unlikely conditions

Put the verbs in brackets into the correct form of the conditional.

Dear Lucy,

I hear you're coming next year to study in Ireland! I thought I'd write and let you know what you can expect from life here.

First, accommodation. If I (1) ..*were*... (be) you, I (2) .... (stay) with a family. Irish people are kind and welcoming. And if you (3) .... (stay) in a small town, you will be amazed at how friendly the people are.

Now, about the weather. You (4) .... (get) very wet here unless you (5) .... (bring) your umbrella – it rains a lot here! I love walking in the beautiful countryside, but I (6) .... (not/able) to go outdoors some days if I (7) .... (not have) a waterproof jacket and trousers to put on.

I (8) .... (not/spend) all my time in Dublin, if I (9) .... (be) you. I have to be in Dublin because I'm studying at the university, but if I (10) .... (have) the choice, I (11) .... (prefer) to stay in a small town in the West of Ireland. I (12) .... (send) you some addresses to write to, if you (13) .... (like).

It's a shame you can't come over sooner. If you (14) .... (come) now, I (15) .... (take) you around in my car, but never mind – I'm sure we'll be able to spend time together next year.

Love,
Anna

3 Structural cloze

Read the text below and think of the word which best fits each space. Use only one word in each space. There is an example at the beginning (0).

A FAMILY ARGUMENT

I get on fairly well with my parents. However, last night we had one of (0) ..*the*.. worst quarrels we've had for years! It was my brother (1) .... started the trouble. He asked me if he (2) .... borrow my Walkman and when I refused he just went into my bedroom and took it. When I complained to Mum, she told (3) .... not to be so childish. She said I ought to be a bit (4) .... generous!

I was annoyed but I didn't say any more. I went upstairs to finish my home-work, (5) .... I thought would take about an hour. After that, I planned to go out. My friends had suggested (6) .... to a disco and I had agreed to meet (7) .... there. The disco is quite a long way away so I knew I would be home (8) .... than usual. I thought I (9) .... better ask Dad if that would be okay. He usually (10) .... me do what I want, because he knows I'm not as irresponsible (11) .... my brother. But this time he refused (12) .... allow me to go out alone. He wanted me to go to the disco with my brother! He said that (13) .... I agreed to go with him, I couldn't go at all! We had a terrible argument. The (14) .... I protested, the angrier he became. In the end, he ordered me to go to my bedroom, (15) .... I spent a very boring evening. I have not forgiven my brother yet!

4 Lexical cloze

Read the text below and decide which answer A, B, C or D best fits each space. There is an example given at the beginning (0).

0 **A** normal **B** usual **C** ordinary **D** natural

THE PRICE OF FAME

Charlotte Church looks like a (0) ....A....... teenager, but she is far from average. She has an amazing voice. Her fans stand in (1) .... for hours to get tickets for her concerts and she is often on television. Charlotte's singing (2) .... began when she performed on a TV show at the age of 11. The head of a record company was so impressed by her voice that he (3) .... her up on the spot. Her first album rose to number one in the charts.

Charlotte still attends school in her home town when she can. (4) .... , she is often away on tour for weeks at a time. She doesn't miss out on lessons, though, because she takes her own tutor with her! She (5) .... three hours every morning with him. Her exam results in all the (6) .... she studies are impressive.

But how does she (7) .... with this unusual way of life? She (8) .... that she has the same friends as before. That may be true, but she can no longer go into town with them because everybody stops her in the street to ask for her (9) .... It seems that, like most stars, she must learn to (10) .... these restrictions and the lack of privacy. It's the price of fame!

1	**A** rows	**B** queues	**C** ranks	**D** files
2	**A** profession	**B** job	**C** labour	**D** career
3	**A** signed	**B** wrote	**C** made	**D** picked
4	**A** Although	**B** While	**C** For	**D** However
5	**A** takes	**B** utilises	**C** spends	**D** uses
6	**A** titles	**B** materials	**C** subjects	**D** lessons
7	**A** cope	**B** adjust	**C** bear	**D** tolerate
8	**A** denies	**B** refuses	**C** insists	**D** complains
9	**A** signature	**B** autograph	**C** sign	**D** writing
10	**A** look down on	**B** make do with	**C** put up with	**D** run out of

5 Word formation

Read the text below. Use the word given in capitals below the text to form a word that fits in the space in the text. There is an example at the beginning (0).

BARGAIN HUNTING

Even people who are not (0) ...*particularly*... keen on shopping would enjoy a trip to our local market. It is a very (1) .... place and is very popular with the tourists who visit the town. (2) .... most markets, this one doesn't sell any food. Instead, there is the most amazing (3) .... of antiques, hand-carved objects, and second-hand clothes! Things are (4) .... cheap, so you can pick up some real bargains. I've bought some of my favourite (5) .... there, including a painting that cost almost nothing but turned out to be extremely (6) .... The only problem about shopping here is that it is hard to resist the (7) .... to buy more than you could (8) .... want! I've had quite a few (9) .... with my family on this topic. They just don't understand the (10) .... I get from finding a real bargain!

(0) PARTICULAR	**(6) VALUE**
(1) COLOUR	**(7) TEMPT**
(2) LIKE	**(8) POSSIBLE**
(3) VARY	**(9) ARGUE**
(4) BELIEVABLE	**(10) ENJOY**
(5) POSSESS	

7 Fitness

Vocabulary ▶ CB Reading 1 pp.78–79

1 Word formation

Use the correct form of the word in capitals at the end of each sentence to fill the gap.

1 My best friend is great fun but he's also very ....! **MOOD**
2 I know that spiders are harmless and my fear is .... but I can't help it! **RATIONAL**
3 I am always so busy that .... is never a problem for me. **BORED**
4 Everybody gets .... before taking an important exam. **ANXIETY**
5 I'm afraid the advice your uncle gave me was rather .... **HELP**
6 Tanya's attempts to win the competition ended in .... **FAIL**
7 The crowd watched with .... as the race began. **EXCITE**
8 The students listened to the counsellor in .... **SILENT**

2 Prepositional phrases

Complete the phrases in *italics* with a word from the list.

pressure / ordinary / proportion / tears

1 My sister had a fight with her boyfriend and came home *in* ....
2 My dad is *under a lot of* .... at work.
3 Try not to let your problems get *out of* .... I'm sure they're not as bad as they seem.
4 Martin arrived after the wedding had started, but that's nothing *out of the* .... – he's always late!

3 Verb + preposition collocations

<u>Underline</u> the correct preposition from the options given in *italics*.

1 Don't worry *for/about* me. I'll be alright!
2 My brother has a lot of problems to cope *with/in* at work.
3 I wish you wouldn't argue *to/with* me all the time!
4 I was so nervous about taking part in the competition that it stopped me *from/in* sleeping.
5 With help, you can learn to deal *in/with* all your problems successfully.

Grammar and Use of English

▶ CB pp.80–81, grammar files 21, 23

1 The passive

Put the verbs in brackets into the passive. Make sure you use the correct tense.

1 Aromatherapy *is believed* (believe) by many people to relieve stress.
2 When we arrived, we found that the class .... (cancel) some time earlier.
3 I .... (tell) many times by my doctor that I must relax more.
4 Relaxation classes .... (hold) every afternoon next week.
5 At this very moment, my brother .... (interview) for a new job.
6 The results of the competition .... (announce) yesterday.
7 We think the new sports centre .... (open) by the headmaster next week.
8 Oh, no. Look! The swimming pool .... (close). We can't go swimming today.
9 The ambulance broke down while my brother .... (take) to hospital.
10 Students .... (give) information about stress busters last month.

2 *need to do* or *need doing*?

> **!** *need* **with passive meaning**
>
> Note the difference in meaning:
> - *need* + *to*-infinitive:
>   *I need to do* some exercise. (= It is necessary.)
> - *need* + *-ing*
>   *My hair needs cutting.* (= My hair needs to be cut.)

Put the verbs in brackets into the correct form, *to*-infinitive or *-ing*.

1 I'm going to the supermarket because I need
   ...*to buy*... (buy) some shampoo.
2 Dad's gone to the garage because his car needs
   .... (service).
3 You should go to the optician's. I think your eyes
   need .... (test).
4 Paul's gone home because he needs .... (go)
   to bed early tonight.
5 Your jacket needs .... (wash) – it's filthy dirty!
6 I'll need .... (study) every night if I want to
   pass this exam.
7 I think my nails need .... (cut) – they're
   getting very long.
8 If you want to go on the excursion, you need
   .... (get) permission from your parents.
9 Do you need .... (have) a letter from the
   doctor if you have a day off school?
10 Don't you think your dress needs ....
   (lengthen)? It's very short.

3 Infinitive forms in the passive

grammar file 21

We can put **present** and **past infinitive** forms into
the **passive** in the following ways:

Active	Passive
1 *Someone ought* **to** *congratulate* the teacher.	*The teacher ought* **to** *be congratulated*.
2 *Someone ought to* *have given* Harry a prize.	*Harry ought to* **have** **been given** a prize.

**Complete the second sentence so that it means the
same as the first.**

1 They ought to give us a holiday.
   We ought ....*to be given*.... a holiday.
2 They must teach students how to relax.
   Students must .... how to relax.
3 They should not put students under too much stress.
   Students should .... under too
   much stress.

4 They may have told Laura to go home early.
   Laura may .... go home early.
5 They could have offered Carlos better advice.
   Carlos could .... better advice.
6 They ought to have warned us about the danger.
   We ought .... about the danger.
7 They should have discussed the problem in more detail.
   The problem .... in more detail.
8 They may offer us aromatherapy classes.
   We may .... aromatherapy classes.

4 Transformations

**Complete the second sentence so that it has a similar
meaning to the first sentence, using the word given.
Do not change the word given. You must use between
two and five words, including the word given.**

1 Everyone thinks Sara will pass the exam. **expected**
   Sarah ....*is expected to*.......... pass the exam.
2 Teenagers aren't buying as many videos these days.
   bought
   Not so many videos ....
   these days.
3 Your bandage needs changing every day. **has**
   Your bandage .... every day.
4 They are treating my dad for stress. **treated**
   My dad .... for stress.
5 You need to fix the bike before you ride it. **fixing**
   The bike .... before you
   ride it.
6 They are going to publish the new book next year.
   published
   The new book .... next year.
7 My parents forced me to pay for the broken window.
   made
   I .... for the broken window
   by my parents.
8 Teams of experts were discussing the problem.
   discussed
   The problem .... teams of
   experts.
9 My parents didn't let me go to the disco. **allowed**
   I .... to the disco.
10 They should have done the work yesterday. **been**
   The work .... yesterday.

5 Relative pronouns ▶ grammar file 23

▶▶ exam tip!

In **Paper 3**, **Part 2** (structural cloze), pay attention to gaps between nouns and verbs, especially if these occur in phrases between commas. You may have to supply a relative pronoun: **who, whom, which, that, whose.**

Complete these sentences with a relative pronoun.

1 Did you see .....*who*..... won the tennis match yesterday?

2 They gave the prize to the boy .... tried hardest during the year.

3 The race, ... was postponed because of the weather, will be held tomorrow.

4 I prefer sports .... are not competitive.

5 The youngest competitor in the Olympics, about .... so much was written in the newspapers, won a gold medal.

6 Mr Jackson, ... daughter was chosen to represent the country in the swimming competition, was very proud.

6 Structural cloze

Read the text below and think of the word which best fits each space. Use only one word in each space. There is an example at the beginning (0).

HOW TO BEAT EXAM STRESS

Are you experiencing the sort of stress (0) .....*that*..... always accompanies examinations? If you are the type of student (1) .... sits at home and panics, stop now! Follow this advice and you will not need (2) .... worry any more.

First, think about time management. A balance (3) .... to be kept between work and play, and this (4) .... be achieved if you plan ahead. A (5) .... weeks before the exam, get some past papers. They will show you the types of questions which (6) .... usually asked. Practise answering the questions in the time which (7) .... allowed in the exam.

Remember that your revision time (8) .... be spent productively. It is silly to listen to music (9) .... is loud and distracting while studying! Work out a sensible schedule and give yourself targets each day (10) .... you can tick off when they (11) .... completed.

Remember that even if there is a lot of work to be (12) ...., other activities should (13) .... be neglected. Research has (14) .... done into the time anyone can study properly without a break. It seems that 40 minutes is the maximum time. Leave yourself time to play games, visit friends and relax. That way, your brain (15) .... be fresh when you return to your studies.

Vocabulary

▶ CB Reading 2 pp.84–85

1 Sports and equipment

1 Match each activity in Column A with the right set of equipment in Column B.

A	B
1 motorbike racing	a) gloves, punchbag
2 tennis	b) net, whistle, boots
3 ice hockey	c) flippers, goggles
4 boxing	d) helmet, goggles, gloves
5 football	e) stick, skates, net
6 diving	f) racquet, net

2 Label the items in the pictures below.

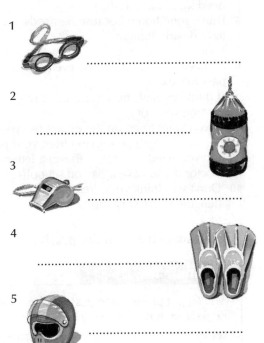

1 ....

2 ....

3 ....

4 ....

5 ....

2 Verb + noun collocations

<u>Underline</u> **the correct verb from the options given in *italics*.**

1 I want to win the race next week so I've got to *do/make* a lot of training.

2 My brother *uses/spends* his time training in the gym.

3 *Take/Make* my advice and give up motor racing; it's much too dangerous.

4 Please *pay/give* attention to what I'm saying!

5 I'm going to *do/make* an effort to get up early and go to the gym.

6 Peter *goes/does* running after school every day.

Vocabulary and Use of English ► CB pp.86–87

1 Word formation

Study the information in the box, then do the exercise below.

> ### Abstract nouns
>
> We can form many **abstract nouns** in the following ways:
>
> | | |
> |---|---|
> | adjective + **-ness** | e.g. kind**ness**, happi**ness** |
> | adjectives + **-ant/-ent** (these drop the final 't' and add **-ce**) | e.g. important – importan**ce**, patient – patien**ce** |
> | verb + **-ment** | e.g. equip**ment** |
> | verb + **-ance** or **-ence** | e.g. annoy**ance**, exist**ence** |
> | verb + **-ion, -sion** or **-tion** | e.g. promote – promot**ion**, decide – deci**sion** |
> | verb + **-al** | e.g. dismiss**al** |
> | verb + **-ing** | e.g. train**ing** |
> | number + **-th** (except 1, 2, 3) | e.g. ten**th** |

Complete the gaps in the following table.

Verb	Adjective	Noun
1 develop	developing developed	development
2 xxxxxxxxxxxx	innocent	....
3	disappointed disappointing	....
4	surviving	....
5 empty	....	emptiness
6	exciting excited	....
7 xxxxxxxxxxxx	....	politeness
8 persuade	....	....

2 Word formation

Study the information in the box, then do the exercise that follows.

> ### Nouns ending in -th
>
> We can form nouns:
>
> - by adding **-th** to certain verbs/adjectives e.g. grow – grow**th**, warm – warm**th**.
> - by adding **-th** to adjectives that describe size and measurements, such as **long**, **high**, **deep**, **strong**, **broad**, **wide**. Be careful! You may have to make other changes to the adjective too e.g. broad – brea**dth**.

Use the correct form of the word in capitals at the end of each sentence to fill the gap.

1 In some places, the river reaches a .... of 30 cms. **DEEP**
2 You need tremendous .... to be an Olympic weight-lifter. **STRONG**
3 He swam the .... of the pool in record time. **WIDE**
4 I hope the new race track is the correct .... **LONG**

3 Word formation

Read the text below. Use the word given in capitals below the text to form a word that fits in the space in the text. There is an example at the beginning (0).

> ### AN OLYMPIC PIONEER
>
> Participating in sport is an excellent way to stay (0) ...*healthy*.. . At the end of the (1) .... century, a man called Coubertin, who was a keen sportsman, put forward a (2) .... to revive the Olympic Games, which had last been held 1,500 years before. People weren't at all (3) .... about his idea at first, but at a (4) .... which was held in Paris in 1894 his proposal was reconsidered. This time it was received with great (5) .... Just two years later, after a great deal of (6) ...., the first modern Olympic Games were held in Athens. It was Coubertin's (7) .... to introduce the (8) .... distinctive five-ring symbol. In 1896, more than 60,000 people bought tickets, on (9) .... of the modest sum of two drachmas! Anyone could be a (10) ....; in fact, some of the spectators took part.

(0) HEALTH	**(4)** CONFER	**(8)** HIGH
(1) NINETEEN	**(5)** EXCITE	**(9)** PAY
(2) PROPOSE	**(6)** PLAN	**(10)** COMPETE
(3) ENTHUSIASM	**(7)** DECIDE	

Reading: *multiple matching (headings)*

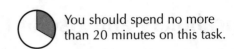 You should spend no more than 20 minutes on this task.

You are going to read a newspaper article about fitness training for footballers. Choose the most suitable heading **A–H** for each part (**1–6**) of the article. There is one extra heading which you do not need to use. There is an example at the beginning (**0**).

A	A break with tradition
B	A chance to make a good impression
C	Gradual acceptance
D	An established idea
E	A fortunate coincidence
F	A positive first response
G	Comparing approaches
H	Under expert guidance

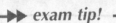 **exam strategy**   Paper 1, Part 1 ▶ CB p.10

▶▶ exam tip!

Always be prepared to go back and check your choices as you work through the matching task. You may want to change your answer. ◀◀

CLUES

Question:

1 This paragraph talks about 'sharing ideas' about methods of training. Which heading expresses this?

2 How did the meeting happen? Was it planned?

3 What training technique does this paragraph describe? How long has this been known by dancers?

4 Is the player in this paragraph in favour of or against the idea? Which heading expresses this?

6 Look for a word in the headings which means the same as 'opportunity'.

First Steps to Fitness

Dance methods are being used to increase the fitness of promising young footballers

| 0 | *H* |

In a room beneath a football stadium in Sheffield, a city in the north of England, the teenagers who hope to be the football stars of tomorrow are dancing up and down, balancing on one leg and performing various steps and hops to the jazz music of Robbie Williams. Dressed in the traditional red and white stripes of the local professional football club, members of the club's youth team are being coached by Jane McClaren, a <u>fully-trained</u> jazz dancer.

| 1 | |

The dance and football programme in Sheffield came about as a result of a meeting between local football coaches and professional dancers. The aim was to share ideas on fitness and training and see how experts in different fields dealt with similar problems. The programme that followed has been so successful that other teams are now considering setting up similar schemes.

| 2 | |

The idea for the meeting came originally from Mileva Drljaca, a specialist in contemporary dance. As she recalls, it happened quite by chance: 'I joined a gym which, it turned out, was also being used by injured players from the local professional football team. As I watched, I realised that some of the training techniques used by ballet dancers might help them towards recovery, and so I mentioned it to their trainer.'

| 3 | |

It is mainly thanks to her suggestion that football clubs are now discovering the concept of the 'strong centre', one familiar to dancers for decades. 'Both traditional and modern dance styles rely on strong stomach muscles,' she explains. 'You can prevent injury to the back and make it loose by having a strong centre. Footballers need a loose back so that they can kick and twist, jump and head the ball, and then land without injury.'

| 4 | |

17-year-old Lewis Killeen, one of the young players, was an instant convert. 'I'm not really into dancing and don't go to discos,' he said. 'But as soon as I started doing it, I could see how it would help. The movements are very similar to those we do in football, especially when you have to turn quickly with the ball.'

| 5 | |

According to the club's trainer, however, the initial reaction of most players to the new idea was more cautious. Some of them were obviously worried that they might be laughed at. But having tried it, most began to see the advantages of the programme. 'They realise there are benefits to be gained from other disciplines,' he said. 'And anything that improves balance, co-ordination and overall fitness must be a good thing.' Young players at the club are now also being taught rock climbing and swimming as an extension of the scheme.

| 6 | |

Meanwhile, back at the stadium, the youth team players are training hard. They are going to perform their dance routine at half-time when Sheffield play an important match next month. It will be the first opportunity they've had to run on to the pitch in front of all the club's fans, and they are keen not to put a foot wrong.

Grammar ▶ CB p.89, grammar file 24

1 Purpose clauses

1 Match the sentence halves to make logical sentences.

1 He went to the gym	a) in order that they would be really fit for the race.
2 I had to phone twice in	b) to do some weight-training.
3 My parents gave me some money	c) order to book the tickets.
4 We left the house early	d) so that I could buy some new trainers.
5 The coach gave my friends extra training	e) so as not to be late for the match.

2 Rearrange the words to make correct sentences.

1 I swim the went a for to pool

....

2 she so be home not late to ran as

....

3 we order queues in arrived to the early avoid

....

4 they to some aerobics gym went the to do

....

5 we hard would so ready race trained for that we be the

....

6 he would that not be phoned parents so they worried his

....

2 It and There

grammar file

A We can use *it* as a subject:

- **to describe a place:**
  It's a holiday resort. It's quiet and peaceful.
- **to talk about the weather:**
  It's sunny today.
- **to give an opinion:**
  It's great that we won so many Olympic medals.
  It was stupid of you to miss the bus.
- **to introduce an adjective:**
  It is necessary to book tickets in advance.

B We use *there*:

- **to say that something exists:**
  There's a spider in the changing rooms!
- **to mention an event:**
  There's been an accident.
- **with *seems* and *appears* + *to*-infinitive:**
  There seems to be a problem.

Complete the sentences with *It* or *There*.

1 .... aren't many sports facilities in our town.
2 .... is a pity that we haven't got a sports centre.
3 .... have been a lot of requests for a sports centre from the public.
4 .... is essential for everyone to exercise regularly.
5 .... is a well-known connection between regular exercise and good health.
6 .... have been a few meetings recently to discuss what to do.
7 .... appears to be a chance that the council will build a swimming pool in the park.
8 .... is a good idea to build a pool there.

3 Transformations

Complete the second sentence so that it has a similar meaning to the first sentence, using the word given. Do not change the word given. You must use between two and five words, including the word given.

1 He goes jogging every day because he wants to get fit. **order**
He goes jogging every day ....*in order to get*...... fit.
2 I wore a hat to avoid getting sunburnt. **as**
I wore a hat so .... sunburnt.
3 You need to arrive early so that you don't miss any of the races. **necessary**
It .... so that you don't miss any of the races.
4 He joined the sailing club because he wanted to impress his girlfriend. **to**
He joined the sailing club .... his girlfriend.
5 We booked in advance to get good seats. **so**
We booked in advance .... good seats.
6 He trained every day because he wanted to win the race. **in**
He trained every day .... the race.
7 She agreed to compete because she didn't want to disappoint her parents. **not**
She agreed to compete .... her parents.
8 I went to the park because I wanted a walk yesterday. **for**
I went to the park .... yesterday.
9 He managed to make some extra money by coaching athletes. **order**
He coached athletes .... some extra money.
10 Finding a place to train was difficult. **was**
It .... a place to train.

Writing: *informal letter*

1 1 **Read the exam task and answer the questions below.**

> You have recently taken up a new sporting activity and your penfriend Alex wants to hear about it. Write a letter to Alex describing the activity and explaining what you particularly like about it.
>
> Write your letter in 120–180 words in an appropriate style. Do not include any postal addresses.

1 Who will read your letter?
  a) your penfriend
  b) your sports instructor
2 Should the style be:
  a) formal?
  b) informal?

2 The task has two parts. Tick (✓) the two points that you must include in your letter.

a) what made you decide to take up this sport
b) what the activity involves
c) what your instructor is like
d) the best thing about the sport
e) why the sport is popular in your country

▶▶ *exam tip!*
You may mention other points about the sport in your letter as long as you cover the two things that are asked for. However, you should keep to the subject of sport. Don't introduce other topics, e.g. your family, holidays, etc. ◀◀

3 Look at the question again. Which one of the following would not be a suitable activity to write about?
a) golf
b) basketball
c) fishing
d) photography
e) swimming

2 Tick (✓) the most suitable content for each paragraph of your letter.

Paragraph 1
a) news about your family
b) thank Alex for his/her letter and introduce the sport
c) news about your school

Paragraph 2
a) the history of the sport
b) what taking part in the sport involves
c) how popular the sport is in your country

Paragraph 3
a) describe a game or match you have enjoyed watching
b) say why you like the sport
c) say which aspect of the sport you enjoy most

Paragraph 4
a) invite Alex to come and take part in the sport
b) arrange to go on holiday with Alex
c) tell Alex about your exams

3 Now write your letter. Remember to:
● write a suitable greeting and ending.
● use informal style.
● cover both parts of the task.
● divide your letter into paragraphs.

4 Check your work.
● Have you completed the task?
● Is the style appropriate?
● Have you used a good range of vocabulary and structures?
● Are the grammar and spelling correct?

8 Travel

Vocabulary ▶ CB Reading 1 pp.90–91

1 Word formation

Use the correct form of the word in capitals at the end of each sentence to fill the gap.

1 My favourite hobby is .... **DIVE**
2 I'd like to study the .... of gorillas in the wild. **BEHAVE**
3 We visited an island which was .... beautiful. **EXCEPTION**
4 Unless there is a great deal of .... in the weather, we'll have to go home! **IMPROVE**
5 Our leader has a detailed .... of the local area. **KNOW**
6 I enjoyed the holiday because it was really .... **RELAX**

2 Prepositions and prepositional phrases

Underline the correct preposition from the options given in *italics*.

1 Why don't you sit *in/under the sunshine* for a while?
2 I'm going *for/on holiday* next week.
3 I didn't speak to the other people in the hotel much because we had nothing *on/in common*.
4 I think French food is the best *in/on the world*.
5 I'm sure it's not *good on/for you* to work so hard; you should take a holiday.
6 We set off *at/in daybreak*.
7 It's no fun travelling *by/on your own*.
8 When we reached our hotel, we were *divided into/ in groups*.

3 Verb + noun collocations

Complete the collocations below with a verb from the list. The noun is in *italics* to help you.

learn / make / spend / take

1 Sergio seems to .... all his *money* on expensive holidays.
2 I've been working hard so I'm going to .... a *break* now.
3 Wherever Paul goes, he always seems to .... new *friends*.
4 I like going on the sort of holidays where you can .... a new *skill*, like diving or sailing.

Grammar and Use of English

▶ CB pp.92–93, grammar files 2, 26

1 Countable or uncountable nouns?

1 Write the nouns in the box in the correct column.

> ~~tourist~~ ~~weather~~ vacancy fun advice trip information ticket peace traffic person luggage help suitcase restaurant shopping problem

Countable nouns	Uncountable nouns
tourist	*weather*
....	....
....	....
....	....
....	....
....	....
....	....
....	....
	....

2 Complete these sentences with *a/an*, *some* or *any*.

1 Can you give me .... advice please?
2 They haven't told us .... details about their holiday yet.
3 I'd like .... fruit, please.
4 The plane trip is going to be .... long one.
5 I'm trying to find .... peace and quiet!
6 Would you like .... help with that suitcase?
7 We've got .... aunt who lives in Australia.
8 There wasn't .... water in the pool!
9 I haven't got .... travel plans at the moment.
10 Have you got .... passport?

2 *so* and *such*

grammar file 26

A so + adjective/adverb (+ *that*-clause)
1 I'm **so** tired – I've had a really long journey.
2 We stayed at the beach **so** long **that** we got sunburn.

B such (a) (+ adjective) + noun (+ *that*-clause)
1 It was **such a** beautiful holiday (that I didn't want to leave)!
2 There were **such** high mountains to climb!
3 We had **such** lovely weather.

<u>Underline</u> the correct choice from the options given in *italics*.
1 I don't know why our guide became *so/such* angry.
2 We had to get a taxi because we had *such a/such* heavy luggage.
3 I don't know why you stayed in *such an/such* awful hotel.
4 The restaurant was *so/such* noisy that I couldn't hear anyone.
5 I never realised dolphins were *so/such* friendly animals.
6 I don't think we've ever met *such/such a* helpful people before.
7 I didn't realise elephants were *so/such* big.
8 Our guide was *so/such* a nice man.

3 *much, many, (a) few* or *(a) little?*

grammar file 2

A (a) few + countable nouns
Notice the difference:
1 The sun was shining so there were **a few** people on the beach.
   (= some people)
2 It was raining so there were **few** people on the beach.
   (= not many people)

B (a) little + uncountable nouns
Notice the difference:
1 There's **a little** hope of finding survivors (= some hope), so the
   search is going to continue.
2 There's **little** hope of finding survivors (= not much hope), so they
   have stopped the search.

Complete these sentences with *much, many, few/a few* or *little/a little.*
1 I'm sorry but I've got very .... money left.
2 We've got .... time left so we can stay and look at the castle,
   if you like.
3 How .... tickets did you buy?
4 I've got .... bananas left. Would you like one?
5 The boat has got a large hole in it so there's .... hope of
   sailing it today, I'm afraid.
6 I prefer it when there aren't .... people on the beach.
7 Would you like .... suntan cream? It's very good.
8 I managed to buy .... really nice souvenirs on holiday.

4 Determiners and quantifiers

<u>Underline</u> the correct word or expression from the options given in italics.
1 I don't mind whether we go on a beach or a wildlife holiday.
   Either/Neither would be great!
2 *Both/Each* of my parents can dive, so we had a wonderful diving holiday.
3 I can neither swim *nor/or* dive, so I didn't enjoy the underwater safari.
4 The guide gave *each/every* of us a leaflet.
5 There were a *great deal of/plenty of* young people in our resort.
6 I don't want to go on *any/some* of the holidays they advertise in that brochure.
7 *None/Neither* of the two guides spoke the local language.
8 We didn't like the hotel and we didn't like the resort, *either/neither*!

5 Extra word: *articles*

➤➤ *exam tip!*

In **Paper 3**, **Part 4** (error correction), pay special attention to articles before nouns. Some of these articles may not be necessary.

• There is no indefinite article **(a/an)** in front of uncountable nouns: *I need ~~an~~ advice.*

• There is no definite article (**the**) in front of general nouns: *I'm very interested in ~~the~~ wildlife.*

• In certain **fixed** phrases the article is omitted: *He's **on** ~~the~~ holiday now.*

◄◄

Two of the sentences below are correct. Tick them (✓). The other sentences contain one unnecessary word. Cross out the words.
1 I love the nature.
2 Please hurry! I need a help.
3 I'm tired. I'm going to the bed.
4 I'm looking for work.
5 I've got the permission to stay at home today.
6 Don't talk such a rubbish!
7 Bill's at work now.
8 I hate the homework!

6 Error correction

Read the text below and look carefully at each line. Some of the lines are correct, and some have a word which should not be there. If a line is correct, put a tick (✓) in the space by the number. If the line has a word which should not be there, write the word in the space. There are two examples at the beginning (0 and 00).

AN UNWELCOME VISITOR

0	✓	I always go on holiday with a few friends. We normally go to Spain
00	*a*	because they have such a wonderful weather there. However my
1	......	friends are keen on the wildlife, so we decided to go to Africa
2	......	this year. The journey was little tiring so we hoped to go to
3	......	the bed as soon as we reached our hotel. However, we soon
4	......	realised there was a little hope of this. Our host had organised a
5	......	welcome party for us! Most of guests stayed until 2 a.m., but we
6	......	had to stay until daybreak. By the time I got to bed, I
7	......	wasn't hardly able to keep my eyes open. I got into bed;
8	......	I was sure I would fall asleep as soon as my head touched
9	......	the pillow. I had no such a luck! I had just closed my eyes when
10	......	I heard a strange noise. I switched on the light. A snake was
11	......	crawling through the open window. There wasn't many time
12	......	to think! It was heading straight towards me! Few of snakes are
13	......	poisonous of course and this one was a harmless grass snake.
14	......	But I didn't know that at the time. I was so absolutely terrified!
15	......	I jumped out of bed and began to scream for the help.

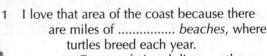

Vocabulary ▶ CB Reading 2 pp.96–97

1 Word formation

Use the correct form of the word in capitals at the end of each sentence to fill the gap.

1 We had to walk through the jungle for hours and the .... was tremendous. **HOT**
2 The trees offered us some .... from the sun. **PROTECT**
3 The hotel guests chatted .... as they waited for dinner. **HAPPY**
4 There is a lot of .... among tourists about the wildlife they see. **IGNORE**
5 My sister wants a career in .... **TOURIST**
6 The .... of the island were very friendly to us. **INHABIT**

2 Adjective + noun collocations

Complete the collocations below with an adjective from the list. The nouns are in *italics* to help you.

family-run / high / natural / protected / sandy / working

1 I love that area of the coast because there are miles of .... *beaches*, where turtles breed each year.
2 Go on safari and discover the beauty of the .... *world*.
3 Alex went on a .... *holiday*, picking fruit in Spain.
4 On our holiday, we stayed at a small .... *hotel* where they made us very welcome.
5 If you go on holiday in .... *season*, all the resorts are bound to be crowded.
6 The tiger is a .... *species* so it is illegal to shoot them.

Vocabulary and Use of English ▶ CB pp.98–99

▶ CB pp.98–99

┌─────────────────────────────┐
➤➤ *exam tip!*

In **Paper 3**, **Part 1** (lexical cloze), you are often tested on your knowledge of dependent prepositions, e.g.:
*The tourists **insisted on** taking photos.*
◀◀
└─────────────────────────────┘

For exercises 1 – 3 , fill the gaps with a suitable preposition. Use your dictionary to help you.

1 Verb + preposition

1 We succeeded ......*in*...... finding a room for the night.
2 He stared .... the receptionist in surprise.
3 The guest complained .... everything in the hotel.
4 I object .... sharing my room with a stranger.
5 You can't depend .... planes to be on time.
6 Please excuse me .... disturbing you.

2 Adjective + preposition

1 famous .....*for*......
2 interested ....
3 proud ....
4 different ....
5 sorry .... / ....
6 bored ....
7 satisfied .... / ....
8 nervous .... / ....

3 Noun + preposition

1 I have a good relationship ....*with*..... my parents.
2 Thanks .... your help.
3 There's been a huge increase .... tourism in that area.
4 Congratulations .... winning the prize!
5 This cream offers complete protection .... sunburn.
6 That airline company has an excellent reputation .... safety.
7 I would like more advice .... eco-holidays.
8 Our guide is an expert .... birds.

4 Lexical cloze

Read the text below and think of the word which best fits each space. Use only one word in each space. There is an example at the beginning (0).

0 A hoping **B** planning **C** dreaming **D** wanting

WATCH THAT TIGER!

Last year I did something I had been (0) .*C*. of for ages. I took a month off work and (1) ..... a flight for India. I (2) ..... for the Kazranga National Park, which is famous (3) ..... its rhinos. A friend had described the wildlife that lives in this park. When he listed the animals you could see, I (4) ..... him of exaggerating; then he showed me the photos. After that, I could talk about nothing but my trip to India. I (5) ..... all my savings on the plane ticket.

I (6) ..... at a forest lodge, (a relaxed sort of hotel) along with many other holiday-makers. On the first morning I and my fellow (7) ..... joked about seeing buffalo and tigers behind (8) ..... bush. We spent the morning riding through the park on elephants. We had marvellous (9) ..... of buffalo and rhino. In the afternoon our guide (10) ..... to take us out again in his jeep. He stopped by a lake so we could (11) ..... photos of some deer. 'There's a tiger,' somebody whispered. 'Don't be silly,' we shouted at her. Our guide had (12) ..... us there was no (13) ..... of seeing a tiger. But the woman was right. The tiger was lying in the long grass, staring at us. We could (14) ..... believe our luck! We were just (15) ..... on the best place to stand to take photographs, when the tiger attacked.

	A		B		C		D	
1	A booked		B took		C paid		D rented
2	A went		B headed		C set		D arrived
3	A in		B by		C for		D on
4	A blamed		B accused		C scolded		D warned
5	A spent		B gave		C bought		D utilised
6	A lived		B remained		C reposed		D stayed
7	A comrades		B colleagues		C guests		D mates
8	A all		B most		C both		D every
9	A looks		B visions		C views		D sights
10	A insisted		B offered		C desired		D suggested
11	A make		B do		C take		D acquire
12	A warned		B said		C denied		D refused
13	A luck		B chance		C reason		D opportunity
14	A almost		B nearly		C never		D hardly
15	A working		B deciding		C discussing		D finding

Reading: *gapped text*

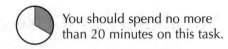

You should spend no more than 20 minutes on this task.

You are going to read an article about some examples of ancient painting which are found on the walls of caves in a remote part of Africa. Six sentences have been removed from the article. Choose from the sentences **A–H** the one which fits each gap (**1–6**) There is one extra sentence which you do not need to use. There is an example at the beginning (**0**).

Art of Ancient Times

Tom Barber went to Africa in search of some very ancient paintings.

I had come to this mountainous part of Africa hoping to see ancient cave art, and here I was looking at a series of caves in the face of the rock. The caves were neither deep nor dark and were well-lit by the morning sun, but I was having trouble finding any of the paintings that the guidebook described. I looked down at the red-dotted line on the hand-drawn map in the book. Nearby, on a rock, a footstep marked in white paint told me I was on the right track, but not how far I was along it. **0** **H**

Looking back at the cliff, there was no sign of the picture I was supposed to be seeing, so I turned back to the guidebook. 'When you've finished your study of these remarkable walls,' it stated, 'turn to the left-hand part of the cave. You will immediately catch sight of an exceptionally clear and delightfully painted hunting scene. I looked to my left. Nothing. But as I looked more carefully, I started to make out a few shapes. **1**

The images were faint and they faded into natural stains on the rock. But it was ancient art and I'd found it. It looked nothing like the illustrations in the guidebook, but I didn't mind. The search had given me an excuse to stop

and take in the natural beauty of the mountains.

I continued walking. After 50 metres, I spotted another white-painted footstep on the rock. **2** This image, like the painting of the hunters, was a magical link between the vanished Bushman culture and the wild beauty of the present day.

I felt thrilled. Here I was on a little-known trail, guiding myself through the countryside with the help of a small guidebook, seeing some of southern Africa's finest rock art. **3** I have seen rock art when locals have shown me sites and I have also been led around famous sites by

bored professional guides, but I have never had the chance of exploring an open-air rock gallery on my own. I was free to make my own discoveries.

And amongst these discoveries, the most impressive were a picture of a group sitting round a fire, painted in black, and a picture of a crowd scene, all heads turned towards the sky. **4** They reminded me so much of paintings I did as a child.

All of this in one of South Africa's last frontiers: a semi-desert with dirt roads and cowboys in pick-up trucks. If it rains in these mountains, August and September are very colourful as flowers cover the rocky ground, but this does not happen every year. **5**

Although the marked trail continued, I decided to go back the way I'd come. It was not to be, however. Almost immediately, I lost the path. The painted footsteps that had guided me so far were, perhaps easier to spot from the intended direction. **6** This was the only place in the world where the Rooibos bush, used to make tea, will grow. I'd bought fresh tea in the nearby mountain town that morning, and now I was looking forward to it.

*Rock engravings,
Namibia, Africa*

A I had apparently reached Site five, for there in front of me was a rather badly-drawn quagga.

B Best of all though, there were red handprints, including the tiny prints of a child, that spoke out to me across centuries and across cultures.

C Souvenir hunters, for example, have been known to chip off artworks to take away with them.

D Unworried, I climbed across rocks and fought my way through bushes to make a track of my own, following the riverbed back to the starting point of my walk.

E The art, on the other hand, is always there.

F And what's more, I was doing it alone, a fact that made the experience unique for me.

G Binoculars brought these into sharper focus and there indeed were the yellows and reds of ancient art, and I could see people chasing horned animals.

H I thought I was at the place the map called 'Site five', but in that case I should be seeing a painting of a quagga, a strange animal, half horse, half zebra.

▶▶ *exam strategy*
Paper 1, Part 3 ▶ CB p.34

 exam tip!
Do the easiest gaps first. You will be able to do the difficult gaps more easily when you have eliminated some of the options.

CLUES

Question:

1 The writer is looking for a hunting scene. In which option is one described?

2 Look for a sentence that describes an 'image'.

3 Look at the sentence which follows the gap. Has he done something similar before?

5 Before the gap, he describes something that does not happen every year. Which option contrasts with this?

Grammar ▶ CB p.101

Modal verbs

We can use the following infinitive forms after modal verbs:

- **modal + bare infinitive:**
  We **can/should protect** our environment.

- **modal + be + -ing:**
  We **should be working** harder to prevent pollution.

- **modal + past infinitives:**
  We **could /should have done** more in the past.

- **modal + have been + -ing:**
  We **ought not to have been swimming** in that part of the river.

1 Modal verbs

Complete the second sentence so that it means the same as the first using the verb in brackets.

1 It's important that we all work together to save our planet. (must)
   We *must all work together to save our planet* .

2 The tourists were wrong to leave rubbish about. (shouldn't)
   The tourists ....

3 Those children should do what the guide tells them. (ought)
   Those children ....

4 It wasn't necessary to cut down all those trees but they did. (needn't)
   They ....

5 It is wrong of the men to hunt the animals. (shouldn't)
   The men ....

6 It isn't necessary to build a new road. (need)
   They ....

7 It was possible for us to stop tourists coming to our island, but we didn't. (could)
   We ....

8 We aren't doing enough to protect wildlife. (should)
   We ....

2 Extra word

All of the sentences below contain one unnecessary word. Cross out the words.

1 We should be take more care of our world.
2 Developers ought not to have build so many hotels.
3 The tourists needn't to have disturbed the beaches where the birds were nesting.
4 We could have been done more to save the rainforests from destruction.
5 The holiday company ought to not have advised customers to go to that resort.
6 On our last holiday, we didn't have need to organise our own accommodation.
7 We should all have do more to save endangered species.
8 They ought not to be allow travel companies to overbook resorts.

3 Transformations

Complete the second sentence so that it has a similar meaning to the first sentence, using the word given. Do not change the word given. You must use between two and five words, including the word given.

1 They were forced to close the safari park.
   had
   They ....*had to close*........ the safari park.

2 It wasn't necessary for the tourists to walk through the forest but they did. **walked**
   The tourists .... through the forest but they did.

3 We aren't doing enough to help endangered animals. **be**
   We should .... more to help endangered animals.

4 The children were climbing the trees, which was wrong. **ought**
   The children ....
   climbing the trees.

5 It isn't necessary for them to build a new road. **have**
   They .... build a new road.

6 It is essential for us to regulate tourism more carefully. **must**
   We .... tourism more carefully.

7 It was wrong of you to pick those flowers. **should**
   You .... those flowers.

8 It is important to protect those beaches. **need**
   We .... those beaches.

9 We didn't do enough for wildlife in the past. **have**
   We could .... for wildlife in the past.

10 It wasn't necessary to cut down the forest. **need**
   They .... down the forest.

Writing: *report* ▶ CB pp.88–89

1 **1 Read the exam task and answer the questions below.**

> You have recently visited a tourist attraction near your town and would like to suggest that your school or college organises a day trip there. Write a report for your school describing the tourist attraction and including suggestions for how the day might be organised.
>
> Write a report of 120–180 words in an appropriate style.

1 Who is going to read the report?
   a) your teachers
   b) the manager of the tourist attraction
   c) tourists

2 What do you want the reader to do? Tick (✓) two of the following.
   a) consider taking a group of students to the attraction
   b) go on a private visit to the attraction
   c) understand why your suggestion is a good one
   d) publish your report in a college magazine

3 Should the style be:
   a) informal?
   b) formal/neutral?

2 Underline the points you must cover in your report.

3 Three of the following points should not be included in your report. Cross them out.

a) a funny thing that happened when you were there
b) how much it costs to get in
c) how to get there
d) who you went with
e) what the attraction is
f) what there is to do at the attraction
g) what souvenirs you bought
h) what facilities there are e.g. cafe, shop etc.
i) how you would plan the day

 *exam tip!*
A report should be fairly impersonal. Be careful not to include irrelevant personal details.

2 **1 Which of the following would be the most suitable introduction for your report?**

1
> *This report is based on a survey of students' opinions.*

2
> The purpose of this report is to give information about an attraction that may be suitable for a school visit.

3
> I recently visited a nearby tourist attraction and I think it would be great if we could all go there.

2 Which of the points in Exercise 1.3 should go under each of the following headings?

1 The attraction
....

2 Practical matters
....
....

3 Plans for a trip
....
....

3 Which one of the following points should be in the conclusion?

a) the advantages and disadvantages of choosing this attraction
b) general advice about day trips
c) your recommendation

3 **Now write your report. Remember to:**
- use the correct format.
- use headings for each section.
- keep the style neutral and impersonal.

4 **Check your work.**
- Have you covered both parts of the task?
- Are the grammar and spelling correct?
- Will your readers be able to make a decision?

Progress check 2

Grammar

1 Modal verbs

Underline the correct modal verb in each sentence.

1 You *don't have to/mustn't* book your train ticket in advance, you can buy it on the train.
2 At our school we *have to/should* pay for all our books.
3 Tom admits that he *needn't/shouldn't* have forced the team to train so hard because the players were very tired when they played the match.
4 In the end they *could/were able to* save enough money for a round-the-world trip.
5 The children *need/should* arrive at school at 8 o'clock because the coach leaves at 8.05.
6 You *shouldn't/needn't* eat so many sweets if you want to lose weight.
7 The plane was delayed so they *didn't need to get up/needn't have got up* as early as they did.
8 It's your decision but I think you *must/ought to* take out insurance before you travel.

2 Extra word

Some of the sentences below are correct. Tick them (✓). The other sentences contain one unnecessary word. Cross out the words.

1 You will need to pack all your personal things and much presents for the family.
2 Why don't you give her a jewellery for her birthday?
3 There are still a few inhabitants left on the island.
4 John went to the travel agency to get an information about flights.
5 None of the members of the fitness club were interested in a new reception area.
6 The police tried to find the thieves but there was a very little hope.
7 Many of families move house every two years.
8 There is a need for more green spaces in this area.

3 Patterns after reporting verbs

Fill the gaps with one suitable word.

1 Simon mentioned that he .... not heard from his sister for several weeks.
2 The children felt that the holiday they'd had the .... year had been better.
3 Mary wondered .... she could afford to buy both pairs of shoes.
4 Please can you tell me .... I can find the sports department?
5 I hoped they .... arrive the next day.
6 The teacher suggested .... spend two hours a day on their homework.
7 Her father explained .... he was late because the train was delayed.
8 Something reminded Sally that it .... her mother's birthday the next day.
9 John promised he would come the .... day.
10 Brian recommended that we .... take the bus to the airport.

4 Tenses

Put the verbs in brackets into the correct tense.

1 I .... (know) him for ten years and I still can't predict how he will react.
2 Don't pick that box up in case you .... (hurt) your back.
3 After we .... (be) at the gym for an hour, we went out for a meal.
4 While Tom .... (wait) for the plane, he did some shopping in the airport.
5 The children were very excited because it was the first time they .... (ever/travel) abroad.
6 We .... (look) forward to this trip for a long time.
7 I'll go to the library when I .... (finish) this book.
8 How long .... (you/spend) at the gym last night?
9 Do you think many tourists .... (visit) the festival next year?
10 What .... (you/plan/do) with all the money you got from selling your car?

5 Conditionals

Complete the second sentence so that it means the same as the first.

1 My advice is to take a few days off and rest.
   If I .... take a few days off and rest.
2 Too much exercise might result in muscle strain.
   If you do ....
   .... strain your muscles.
3 Sam is very fit because he goes swimming three times a week.
   If Sam ....
   be so fit.
4 You won't catch the train unless you hurry up.
   If you ....
   .... catch the train.
5 Don't hesitate to ask for anything you need.
   If you .... to ask.

6 *would, used to, be/get used to*

Complete the following sentences using the correct form of *would, used to, be/get used to*.

1 It takes a long time to .... speaking in a foreign language.
2 Before the days of television and radio people .... sit around and tell stories.
3 When you leave home, you will have to .... doing all the washing and cleaning.
4 I .... be able to jump over that fence, but I can't now.
5 This school was very frightening at first but I .... it now.

7 Expressing purpose

Fill the gaps with one suitable word.

1 They went to the travel agency .... book a holiday.
2 Don't go to a big city like London .... a relaxing holiday!
3 Michael bought a new motorbike .... order to get to work more quickly.
4 The council has banned cars from the city centre so .... to make it safer for pedestrians.
5 Schools are occasionally closed for the day in .... that the teachers can attend a training course.

Vocabulary

8 Word formation

1 Complete the table.

	Noun	Verb	Adjective	Negative adjective
1	*replacement*	replace	....	....
2	excess	....	....	xxxxxxx
3	....	attract	....	....
4	....	....	competitive	....
5	....	restore	xxxxxxx	xxxxxxx
6	advice	....	....	....
7	....	....	supervised	....
8	....	....	....	....

2 Use the correct form of the word in capitals at the end of each sentence to fill the gap.

1 The .... of the town centre to the way it was in the nineteenth century will take many years. **RESTORE**
2 She was most upset about the loss of her mother's letters; they were .... **REPLACE**
3 There is going to be a terrible storm tonight and it is .... to stay at home. **ADVICE**
4 Small children should not be allowed to play in the street .... **SUPERVISE**
5 The school computer network cannot cope with .... use. **EXCESS**

9 Choosing the right word

Underline the correct word from the options given in *italics*.

1 The bride had her dress *specially/especially* made for the occasion.
2 Have you ever had a serious *injury/wound* such as a broken leg?
3 When you have finished, please come *straight/direct* home.
4 A healthy diet brings many *benefits/rewards*.
5 It was a very long *travel/journey*, so we decided to go overnight.
6 Can you *change/exchange* a £20 pound note?
7 The best *cure/healing* for a cold is lots of rest.
8 I went to work *despite/although* having a headache.
9 This tooth *hurts/aches* when I eat something cold.
10 Parties are good opportunities to *know/meet* new people.

10 Phrasal verbs

Complete the sentences using the correct form of the phrasal verbs in the box.

drive off	put up with	face up to	check in	hold up

1 I'm sorry I'm late; I was .... in the traffic for half an hour.
2 The robbers jumped into the car and .... at great speed.
3 You should complain because you can't be expected to .... such rudeness from sales staff.
4 It's time to .... the fact that you can't afford to live the way you do.
5 First class passengers don't usually have to queue to .... for their flights.

9 Discoveries

Vocabulary ▶ CB Reading 1 pp.104–105

1 Word formation

Use the correct form of the word in capitals at the end of each sentence to fill the gap.

1 Many people believe in the .... of aliens. **EXIST**
2 However, until now, nobody has produced any .... that intelligent life exists anywhere but on Earth. **PROVE**
3 Many planets are boiling hot or freezing cold and are completely .... to sustain life. **SUIT**
4 Sadly, it is .... that there is intelligent life on any other planet in our galaxy. **LIKELY**
5 People often claim to have seen UFOs but there may be a simple .... for this. **EXPLAIN**
6 However, it seems .... probable that we will discover life in other galaxies one day. **INCREASE**

2 Prepositions

Fill the gaps with a preposition from the list. You will need to use some of the prepositions more than once.

of / from / for / on / with

1 The Earth is the only planet capable .... sustaining life.
2 The heat from the sun prevents all the water on the Earth .... freezing.
3 Who is to blame .... spreading the recent rumours about UFOs?
4 What would you do if you came face to face .... an alien?
5 I am convinced .... the existence of life on Mars.
6 We rely .... the heat from the Sun to warm our planet.
7 You could never convince me .... the existence of UFOs.
8 The conditions on Jupiter and most of the other planets are unsuitable .... life to exist.

Grammar and Use of English

▶ CB pp.106–107, grammar file p.17

1 Modal verbs

<u>Underline</u> the correct verb form from the options given in *italics*.

1 You're joking surely? You *can't/shouldn't* believe in little green men!
2 You've seen an alien? You *can't/mustn't* be serious! You *can/must* be joking!
3 In the future we *must/might* be able to contact other life forms, but we will probably never meet them 'face to face'.
4 There *can't be/hasn't to be* any other planet in our galaxy with the same conditions for life as the Earth.
5 These days, scientists *can/could* send signals thousands of miles into space.
6 There *must/can* be hundreds of other galaxies in the universe.
7 Tom *must/may* have been telling lies when he said he saw a UFO, but we just don't know.
8 Aliens *mustn't/can't* have taken Laura. She's downstairs, watching TV!
9 You *can/must* have lost your wallet. It's not here now.
10 Lisa was at home last night. You *mustn't/can't* have seen her at the police station!

2 Correct the mistakes

Two of the sentences below are correct. Tick them (✓). The other sentences contain mistakes with modals. <u>Underline</u> the mistakes and correct them.

1 You couldn't <u>see</u> a UFO last night. You must have <u>dreamt</u>!

   couldn't have seen

   must have been dreaming

2 They may land astronauts on Mars some time in the future.

   ....

3 Didn't you hear what the police officer said last night? You can't listen.

   ....

4 Maria may be coming to stay with us. She's going to let us know very soon.

   ....

5 Aliens can't try to contact us at the moment, otherwise we would have received signals from them.

   ....

6 I must lose my key! I can't find it anywhere.

   ....

7 Paul says he's been inside an alien spacecraft. He must imagine it!

   ....

8 Stella can't go to Canada this morning. I've just seen her on the beach.

   ....

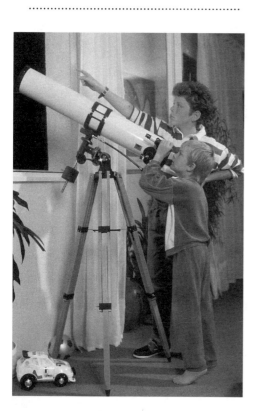

3 Transformations

Complete the second sentence so that it has a similar meaning to the first sentence, using the word given. Do not change the word given. You must use between two and five words, including the word given.

1 I expect you are very tired after your trip. **be**
   You ...*must be*...................... very tired after your trip.

2 It is possible that scientists are not telling the truth. **might**
   Scientists .... the truth.

3 I'm sure it wasn't difficult to solve the mystery. **have**
   It .... easy to solve the mystery.

4 I'm sure Carlos didn't go to work today because his car is outside his house. **gone**
   Carlos .... to work today because his car is outside his house.

5 I suppose they were working all night. **must**
   They .... all night.

6 I don't think they are staying at that hotel because they haven't checked in. **be**
   They .... at that hotel because they haven't checked in.

7 I don't believe the man was captured by an alien. **have**
   The man .... by an alien.

8 It's possible that the spacecraft you saw were spy planes. **could**
   The spacecraft you saw .... spy planes.

9 It is possible that aliens are watching us now! **may**
   Aliens .... us now!

10 It is possible that aliens have visited us in the past. **might**
   Aliens .... in the past.

4 Extra word: *pronouns*

**exam tip!**

In **Paper 3**, **Part 2** (error correction), pay attention to subject and object pronouns, e.g. **I, me, he, him, it, them**. These may be unnecessary.

Two of the sentences below are correct. Tick them (✓). The other sentences all contain one unnecessary pronoun. Cross them out.

1 My father he works as a scientist in a research centre.

2 I like studying Astronomy because it is a very interesting subject.

3 The spacecraft which they sent it to Mars came back with rock samples.

4 My sister discovered her a star that nobody else had seen.

5 The planet it was too distant to see in our telescope.

6 I bought him a telescope for his last birthday and he uses it a lot.

7 The object that some people they thought was a UFO turned out to be a hot-air balloon.

8 My friends and I we are hoping to join the school trip to the Science Observatory next week.

9 The 'alien' that the man thought he saw it turned out to be a motor cyclist in a shiny silver suit!

10 I have a friend whose brother he is an astronaut.

5 Error correction

Read the text below and look carefully at each line. Some of the lines are correct, and some have a word which should not be there. If a line is correct, put a tick (✓) in the space by the number. If a line has a word which should not be there, write the word in the space. There are two examples at the beginning (0 and 00).

Mars at Opposition · February 1995
Hubble Space Telescope · WFPC2

LIFE ON MARS

0	*can*	The question about whether life can exists in other parts of our galaxy
00	✓	may soon be answered. NASA* is to send two robots to look for
1	......	life on the surface of Mars. Scientists they think that Mars might have
2	......	been contained water in the past. If that is proved to be true, experts believe
3	......	it is a sign that some forms of life could have developed on Mars. The
4	......	two robots will land them in different locations. One robot may land on
5	......	a safe, flat area. The second he might be sent to a rockier part of the planet.
6	......	The robots are heavier than 'Sojourner', the last robot sent to Mars, which
7	......	it could travel more than 300 feet a day. Each of the robots will be about
8	......	4 feet high and will weigh about 250 pounds. Although scientists have not
9	......	had decided exactly where the robots should land, they are interested in
10	......	areas where they think water may once have flowed. Sending two robots to Mars
11	......	must to be very expensive. Scientists are hoping that they will have more
12	......	success with this project than they had with a previous one. On that
13	......	occasion the rocket they launched must have been suffered major damage
14	......	during its voyage because it might failed to send signals back to Earth.
15	......	Experts believe it could have had crashed when it landed on the planet.

* NASA = National Agronautics and Space Administration – the US government organisation that is responsible for space travel and exploration.

Vocabulary

▶ CB Reading 2 pp.110–111

1 Choosing the right word

<u>Underline</u> the correct options from the ones given in *italics*.

1 Archaeologists have discovered the remains of a prehistoric human *development/settlement*.
2 A group of walkers *came across/turned out* the site while they were exploring the valley.
3 They *picked/picked up* pieces of clothing and tools and took them to a local museum.
4 Archaeologists found stones that *looked like/seemed* primitive tools.
5 The jewellery found at the site *came across/turned out* to be real gold.
6 They discovered a cloak made of pieces of skin that were *sewn/stuck* together with cotton.
7 The man was buried at a *depth/distance* of one metre under the snow.
8 The body of the man had been *lain/preserved* in the ice.

2 Adjective + noun collocations

Complete the collocations below with an adjective from the list. The noun is in *italics* to help you.

wild / heated / latest / freezing / stone-age

1 The man had probably been killed by a .... *animal*, such as a wolf.
2 How much do you know about the history of .... *man*?
3 Scientists cannot agree about some of the details and so they have had many .... *discussions*.
4 The archaeologists had to work outdoors in the snow and in the .... *cold*.
5 Scientists are very excited about their .... *find* as it will tell us much more about our ancient ancestors.

Vocabulary and Use of English ▶ CB p.112–113

1 Word formation

Study the information in the box, then do the exercises below.

Forming nouns

We can form many nouns by adding these suffixes to all or part of an adjective. There may also be some other spelling changes.

adjective + **-ty**	e.g. *cruel – cruelty*
adjective + **-ity**	e.g. *stupid – stupidity, curious – curiosity*
adjective + **-ility**	e.g. *probable – probability*
adjective + **-ry**	e.g. *brave – bravery*
adjective + **-ty**	e.g. *cruel – cruelty*
adjective + **-cy**	e.g. *private – privacy, fluent – fluency*
adjective + **-y**	e.g. *envious – envy*

Note: Some nouns are irregular, e.g. *poor – poverty*.

---

1 Complete the table below with the appropriate noun.

Adjective	Noun
1 generous	......*generosity*......
2 honest	....
3 creative	....
4 necessary	....
5 able	....
6 scarce	....
7 invisible	....
8 possible	....

2 Use the correct form of the word in capitals at the end of each sentence to fill the gap.

1 The .... of students do not learn much about archaeology at school. **MAJOR**
2 What .... was the scientist who discovered the Egyptian tombs? **NATIONAL**
3 The discovery of the stone-age man received a lot of .... in the national press. **PUBLIC**
4 Archaeologists have found a .... of stone-age tools, hidden under the snow. **VARIOUS**
5 As head of the archaeology team, Miguel is in a position of great .... **RESPONSIBLE**
6 Tanya's promotion caused a great deal of .... among her colleagues. **JEALOUS**
7 There is a strong .... that our ancestors originally came from Africa. **PROBABLE**
8 I'm going to the Egyptian exhibition as soon as I get an .... **OPPORTUNE**
9 Stone-age people lived very different lives to us but there are many ...., too. **SIMILAR**
10 They are interviewing candidates to test their .... for working in this field. **SUITABLE**

2 Word formation

Read the text below. Use the word given in capitals below the text to form a word that fits in the space in the text. There is an example at the beginning (0).

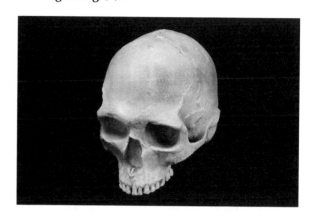

NEANDERTHAL MAN

An important (0) .*discovery*. was made in Germany in 1859. A group of (1) .... found the body of a Neanderthal man. Neanderthals lived 30,000 years ago! They vanished when our ancestors, 'homo sapiens', migrated from Africa to Europe. Originally, scientists believed that Neanderthals were a (2) .... different species. They thought that Neanderthals were primitive cavemen who had no real (3) .... , and that they were (4) .... to use tools or to communicate properly. However, this (5) .... was false. Neanderthals developed (6) .... complex tools. They had good (7) .... skills. They cared for their sick and were respectful in their (8) .... towards each other. So why did the Neanderthals disappear? Maybe the (9) .... of 'homo sapiens' in their territory meant that there was not enough food for them. Another (10) .... is that the two races fought. Maybe Neanderthals were hunted and eventually destroyed by our ancestors.

---

(0) DISCOVER	**(6) SURPRISING**
(1) SCIENCE	**(7) COMMUNICATE**
(2) COMPLETE	**(8) BEHAVE**
(3) INTELLIGENT	**(9) ARRIVE**
(4) ABLE	**(10) POSSIBLE**
(5) ASSUME	

Reading: *multiple-choice questions*

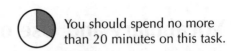

You should spend no more than 20 minutes on this task.

You are going to read a report about a mysterious creature that was sighted in the USA. For questions **1–6**, choose the answer (**A**, **B**, **C** or **D**) which you think fits best according to the text.

Could it be Bigfoot?

Over the years, there have been many sightings in various parts of the world of a mysterious large hairy creature, unknown to science. Although it has never been captured, nor successfully filmed, the creature goes by various names, for example 'Yeti' in Asia and 'Bigfoot' in the USA. I run a website on the Internet where people who think they've caught sight of the **elusive** creature can file a report.

line 8

One of the most interesting reports of recent years involves two men, Steve and Larry (not their real names), who were on a mountain-biking weekend in the state of Washington in the USA. They were riding their bikes up Lookout Mountain near Bellingham. It was 11 a.m. on a warm Sunday and the sky was deep blue. Suddenly Larry braked. As Steve said later, 'I was about to shout at him, but then I saw the look on his face. I knew it was something serious, and then he looked over at me and pointed, and I looked over and there it was.'

What Steve saw was a large two-legged creature, covered with black fur, standing on a log at the bottom of a slope about 20 metres away. The figure was about two metres tall and had its back turned to the men. At first, he presumed it was a bear, a familiar enough sight in that part of the world. It was only in sight for a few seconds before it jumped off the log away from them. 'When it jumped off the log and landed on its rear feet,' explained Steve laughing nervously, 'that's when I knew it was something that I'd never seen before.' The strange figure went down beside the log and disappeared, whether into the bushes or into a crouching position behind the log, the men could not tell. Steve said, 'We both looked at each other and went, "Whoa!"'

The men listened carefully, expecting to hear the creature making its escape through the undergrowth, but there was no rustling in the bushes. They'd heard it land on its feet on the ground, but now there was complete silence. Larry whispered, 'That's odd. It must still be there.' Then they got scared. 'Let's get out of here!' said Steve. The men tore off down the mountain, putting as much distance between themselves and the thing as they could. 'We weren't thinking straight,' explained Steve. 'It never occurred to us to go back and investigate.'

That evening Steve searched the Internet to find a way of reporting the sighting and found me. Fortunately I was free and so able to go back to the scene with Steve and some other friends just a few days later. Steve had got over his experience by then, and Larry had returned to work. Both men are in their late 30s and work as commercial fisher-men in the hazardous waters of the Arctic. Steve is certainly fit and made the bike ride up the mountain look easy. But when we got to within 20 metres of the site, he broke out into a cold sweat and began shaking. 'This is the place,' he said, and there could be little doubt that it matched his earlier description. I looked him square in the eye and called on my seven years' experience as a private investigator. All my instincts told me that his discomfort was genuine.

We found the log and discovered that some moss where the figure had supposedly stood had certainly been disturbed by something. On the other side of the log, there were some large impressions 60 centimetres long on the ground. It was hard to tell what they were, but they certainly weren't bear prints. A few broken branches littered the area. We concluded that something big had been there, but it was impossible to tell what. We combed an area around 1,000 metres square, looking for hair or any other signs, but found nothing further.

1 The word 'elusive' in line 8 describes

   A how difficult it is to find the creature.
   B the creature's physical appearance.
   C how scientists regard the creature
   D the level of interest in the creature.

2 Steve first realised that something was wrong when

   A Larry pointed at something.
   B Larry stopped suddenly.
   C Larry looked at him strangely.
   D Larry shouted something to him.

3 When did Steve realise that he didn't recognise the creature?

   A as soon as he saw it
   B when he saw how tall it was
   C when it started to move
   D after it had disappeared

4 What surprised the men about the creature after it had jumped?

   A the noises it made
   B the place that it landed
   C the fact that it followed them
   D the fact that it didn't run away

5 What did the writer notice about Steve when he returned to the place where he'd seen the creature?

   A He seemed to be cold.
   B He seemed really frightened.
   C He seemed unsure of his story.
   D He couldn't look him in the eye.

6 What conclusions did the writer draw from the evidence at the site?

   A There was no evidence to support Steve's story.
   B A large animal had certainly been there.
   C Most of the evidence had been destroyed.
   D Steve had probably seen a large bear.

---

 exam strategy   Paper 1, Part 2 ▶ CB p.22

 exam tip!

If the multiple-choice question is an incomplete sentence, the whole sentence must match the text. All the options may be true, but only one will match the beginning of the sentence. ◀◀

CLUES

Question:

1 Read Paragraph 1 carefully. Which option best describes the creature?

2 Look for a word in the second paragraph with a similar meaning to 'realise'. Read that part carefully.

5 When they returned, Steve showed certain physical reactions. What do these usually indicate?

Grammar ▶ CB p.115, grammar file 25

1 Participle clauses

Join each pair of sentences using a participle clause.

1 He had missed the last bus. John decided to walk home.
   Having missed.. the last bus, John decided to walk home.
2 She wasn't sure of the way. Sarah stopped and asked a man in the street.
   Not .... sure of the way, Sarah stopped and asked a man in the street.
3 He knew his parents would be worried. John rang them up.
   .... that his parents would be worried, John rang them up.
4 Peter saw something strange in the sky. He ran to get his binoculars.
   .... something strange in the sky, Peter ran to get his binoculars.
5 Clare shook with fear. She stared at the figure in front of her.
   .... with fear, Clare stared at the figure in front of her.
6 They had never seen a UFO before. The police officers stared in astonishment.
   Never .... a UFO before, the police officers stared in astonishment.
7 Laura was terrified. She went towards the space ship.
   Despite .... terrified, Laura went towards the space ship.
8 Sam didn't know what was happening. He approached the 'alien.'
   Not .... what was happening, Sam approached the 'alien.'

2 Error correction

Read the text below and look carefully at each line. Some of the lines are correct, and some have a word which should not be there. If a line is correct, put a tick (✓) in the space by the number. If a line has a word which should not be there, write the word in the space. There are two examples at the beginning (0 and 00).

ALIEN ENCOUNTER

0	*he*	In New Mexico, USA, a police officer called Zamora he was following
00	*✓*	a speeding motorist. While he was driving among the deserted hills near
1	......	the main town, he heard a sudden roar. Looking it round, he saw a blue
2	......	flame in the sky ahead. He left the road and drove up the hill. Then, when
3	......	having spotted something that looked like an overturned car about 150
4	......	metres off the road, he stopped. Getting him out of the car, he went
5	......	to investigate. As he came closer, he saw the 'car' was an oval, silvery
6	......	object on four feet. Two small human-like figures, who wearing white
7	......	clothes that looked as like overalls, were moving around near the
8	......	object. Zamora approached them, because intending to offer them
9	......	some help, but the 'aliens' did not respond. Looking in alarmed, they
10	......	jumped into their mysterious vehicle. Zamora then heard a roar which
11	......	grew up louder and louder. Trembling with fear, the police officer
12	......	turned over and fled. The sighting has never been explained. The US
13	......	Airforce made a statement which suggesting that the UFO may have
14	......	been a test flight. But this seems like improbable, as no man-made
15	......	oval object has ever flown successfully until now.

Writing: *discursive composition* ▶ CB pp.100–101

1 Read the exam task and answer the questions below.

> Your class has recently had a discussion on the advantages and disadvantages of preserving historical buildings. Your teacher has now asked you to write a composition giving your opinion on the following question:
>
> *Should all buildings be knocked down after 50 years?*
>
> Write a composition of 120–180 words in an appropriate style.

1 Who will read your composition?
   a) your class   b) your teacher

2 Should the style be:
   a) informal?   b) neutral/formal?

3 What do you want the reader to be able to do?
   a) make a decision about knocking down old buildings
   b) understand your point of view
   c) list all the advantages and disadvantages of knocking down old buildings

2 1 Look at the following list of ideas and put them in the correct column: 'Points for' or 'Points against'.

a) very old buildings attract tourists
b) old buildings are expensive to keep
c) old buildings help us to learn about the past
d) many old buildings are beautiful
e) we need the space for modern, more practical buildings
f) many old buildings are ugly

Points for	Points against
(a) very old buildings attract tourists	

2 Match the following examples of old buildings to the points in Exercise 2.1. Some will illustrate more than one point.

1 the Parthenon in Athens
2 the Taj Mahal in India
3 the Colosseum in Rome
4 apartment blocks
5 old factories

3 Add examples of places you have been to.

➤➤ *exam tip!*

It is a good idea to illustrate your arguments with examples.
◀◀

3 Make a paragraph plan for your composition.

1 Number the following paragraph topics in a logical order.

☐ a) Reasons why buildings should be knocked down after 50 years. Give examples of buildings it is not worth keeping.
☐ b) Introduce the topic and state my own point of view.
☐ c) Summarise and restate my point of view.
☐ d) Reasons why old buildings should be kept. Give examples.

2 Remember you can:
1 argue in favour OR
2 argue against OR
3 give both sides of the argument.

Which of these options does the above paragraph plan follow?

4 Now write your composition. Remember to:
- state your point of view clearly.
- give examples.
- use linking words to list your arguments.

5 Check your work.
- Have you written in an appropriate style?
- Have you used a range of vocabulary and structures?
- Are the grammar and spelling correct?

10 Technology

Vocabulary ▶ CB Reading 1 pp.116–117

1 Word formation

Use the correct form of the word in capitals at the end of each sentence to fill the gap.

1 I play games on my computer but I am not .... enough to use it for any other tasks. **CONFIDENCE**
2 My lap-top computer is really .... so I take it everywhere with me. **USE**
3 My dad doesn't care what he looks like and always wears .... clothes. **FASHIONABLE**
4 My sister's worst fault is ....; she's always looking at herself in the mirror. **VAIN**
5 The computer I've just bought was .... inexpensive. **RELATIVE**
6 I've been eating a cake, and now my fingers are very .... **STICK**
7 The shop assistant gave me some good .... on which software I should buy. **ADVISE**
8 I find the Internet is a great way to find .... quickly. **INFORM**

2 Choosing the right word

Underline the correct word from the options given in *italics*.

1 Nowadays, a mobile phone is an important fashion *accessory/device*.
2 My sister wears such strange fashions that everyone *glances/stares* at her when she walks down the street.
3 My uncle's flat is full of electronic *gadgets/features*.
4 He's an engineer and he's always coming up with crazy new *accessories/inventions*, like cars that sail on water.
5 When I laughed at his latest idea, he *frowned/grinned* in annoyance.

3 Prepositional phrases

Complete the phrases in *italics* with a word from the list.

date / e-mail / end / Internet / market / whole

1 I wanted a lap-top computer but *in the* .... I bought a desktop computer.
2 A new type of car goes *on the* .... next week.
3 Companies now do a lot of business *over the* .... rather than by post.
4 These days I contact all my friends *by* .... because it's cheaper than the phone.
5 I think computers are a great invention *on the* .... but they do have some drawbacks.
6 Technology is moving very quickly; nowadays computers are *out of* .... only months after you buy them.

Grammar and Use of English

▶ CB pp.118–119

grammar file 5

Future continuous and future perfect

A Position of adverbs

We put adverbs like **already**, **just** and **still** between a modal verb (*will, may* etc.) and a present or past participle:

1 *I may **still** be learning English next year.*
2 *Will you **still** be living in this house in 10 years' time?*
3 *By the time we arrive, they will **just** have finished.*

We normally put **yet** at the end of the phrase.
*She will not have read my letter **yet**.*

B Time expressions

● **+ future continuous**
We often use time expressions like **in two weeks'/a year's time** or **this time next month/year**, with the future continuous tense:
*I'll be living in France **this time next year**.*

● **+ future perfect**
We often use time expressions like **by,** and **by the time (that) + present simple/present perfect**, with the future perfect tense.

1 ***By** Christmas, I will have saved enough money to buy a computer.*
2 *I will have finished my homework **by the time** you get here.*

1 *will do* or *will be doing*?

Put the verbs in brackets into the correct form.

1 Isn't technology marvellous! While you are shopping tomorrow, I ..*will be flying*..... (fly) to Australia.
2 Okay! I promise I .... (not/use) your computer while you're out!
3 Ladies and gentlemen, this is your captain speaking. We .... (take off) in five minutes, as planned, so please fasten your seat belts.
4 Excuse me sir. .... (you/eat) lunch in the hotel today or are you going to the Science Exhibition?
5 I think I .... (give) my parents a ring on my mobile phone. I'm sure they'll be worried about me.
6 I hear you .... (go) to London with your family as usual this summer. .... (you/buy) me a computer game while you're there if I give you the money?
7 I'm afraid I can't go on the Biology trip with you on Wednesday afternoon. I .... (take) my Music exam at that time.
8 .... (you/still/study) in two years' time, or will you have left school?

2 *will have done* or *will have been doing*?

Put the verbs in brackets into the correct form.

1 I ....*will have put*........... (put) all my homework on disc by the time dinner is ready.
2 Will you get up early to finish your homework, do you think, or .... (you/finish) it before you go to bed?
3 They .... (work) on that invention for three years by the time the project finishes.
4 If you don't hurry, the last bus .... (leave) before we get to the bus stop.
5 .... (your group/already/finish) the project by tomorrow, do you think?
6 By this time tomorrow, I .... (just/get) the results of my computer test.
7 By the time I finish work, I .... (type) for three hours without stopping!
8 Do you think robots .... (take over) the world in a hundred years from now?

3 Extra word: *reflexive pronouns*

 *exam tip!*

In **Paper 3**, **Part 4**, you are often tested on your knowledge of reflexive verbs.

grammar file

A Object pronouns
We must use an object after certain verbs such as *enjoy*, *like*, *tell*.
*Do you like **that boy**? I enjoy **dancing**.*

B Reflexive pronouns

Reflexive pronouns such as *myself*, *himself* etc. are not as common in English as in many other languages. Verbs such as: *wake up*, *get up*, *wash*, *shave*, *get dressed*, *relax* are not normally reflexive in English.

1 *I washed ~~myself~~ and got dressed quickly.*
2 *Tom woke ~~himself~~ up early that morning.*

We sometimes (but not always!) use reflexive pronouns:

- with verbs like *cut*, *dry*, *enjoy*, *hurt*, *behave*:
  *I enjoyed **myself** at the party.*
- with certain phrasal verbs like *give yourself up*:
  *The murderer gave **himself** up to the police.*
- in certain expressions:
  *Look after **yourself**! I did all the work **by myself**.*

Six of the sentences below are correct. Tick them (✓). The other sentences contain one unnecessary reflexive pronoun. Cross them out.

1 I hope you enjoy yourself at the party!
2 My brother forgot to shave himself this morning.
3 My friend locked himself out of his house yesterday.
4 I got myself up very late on Sunday morning.
5 Don't eat too much or you'll make yourself sick!
6 I wonder myself if it will rain tomorrow.
7 I don't care what you do. Please yourself!
8 If you're tired, why don't you lie yourself down and have a rest?
9 Don't blame yourself for what happened.
10 My brother has no confidence. He's always putting himself down.

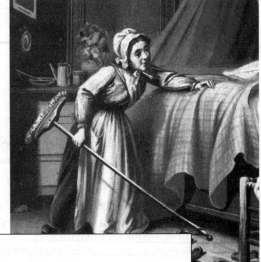

4 Error correction

Read the text below and look carefully at each line.
Some of the lines are correct, and some have a word
which should not be there. If a line is correct, put a
tick (✓) in the space by the number. If a line has a word
which should not be there, write the word in the space.
There are two examples at the beginning (0 and 00).

THE HOME OF THE FUTURE

0	✓	Before the 1800s, few homes had any luxuries. Devices like vacuum
00	*themselves*	cleaners and dishwashers only appeared themselves in the
1	....	1900s. Until then, all housework has had to be done by hand and this took
2	....	a very long time. The home of the future will have be designed to offer its
3	....	inhabitants a secure, comfortable and adaptable environment. Architects
4	....	and engineers will be take advantage of advances in electronics. They will
5	....	create living spaces that can easily be altered by the occupants. Intelligent devices
6	....	will play up an important role in many houses. Robot cleaners and 'smart'
7	....	exercise machines that can monitor health already will be as common as
8	....	today's microwave ovens and washing machines. Experts predict that by
9	....	2025, the average home will have done as much computing power as a nuclear
10	....	power station in the 1990s. Computers will be small and cheap and that
11	....	we will be able to have them everywhere. They will be able to sense
12	....	our presence and adjust the light and temperature automatically, according as
13	....	to our needs. By 2015, designers still will have created furniture that can
14	....	change shape and colour. They may have designed also a robot vacuum
15	....	cleaner which detects dirt and it cleans it up automatically.

Vocabulary ▶ CB Reading 2 pp.122–123

1 Word formation

Use the correct form of the word in capitals at the
end of each sentence to fill the gap.

1 There have been a number of .... from shops in
our village. **THIEF**
2 The number of bank .... in our area has
increased. **ROB**
3 The police are checking the .... of the man's
statement. **ACCURATE**
4 There is a .... of ways in which you can make
your home safer. **VARY**
5 We were worried about our .... so we have
installed a burglar alarm. **SECURE**
6 Nowadays, alarms are more .... than they were
twenty years ago. **RELY**
7 The police must fight crime but they must also protect
the .... of the individual. **FREE**
8 The police can now patrol the streets without being
.... present. **PHYSICAL**

2 Noun + preposition collocations

Underline the correct preposition from the options
given in *italics*.

1 The police have reported a drop *in/on* crime.
2 The police depend on the public to help them in their
fight *with/against* crime.
3 In Britain, there is a demand *about/for* longer prison
sentences to be given.
4 There is a certain amount of conflict *with/between*
the police and football fans.
5 Detectives need witnesses to give them a description
of/from the robbers.
6 My friend got the blame *for/about* breaking the
window but it was not his fault.
7 A police officer is coming to our school to give a talk
in/on crime.
8 The relationship *between/with* the local people and
the tourists is excellent.

3 Collocations with *make* and *take*

Complete the sentences below with the correct form of *make* or *take*.

1 The hijackers have .... a number of hostages.
2 Before we start work, I think we should sit down and .... a plan.
3 I'm just going to get my camera and .... a photograph of you all.
4 Before I left home this evening, I .... a promise that I wouldn't stay out late.
5 The police officer arrived soon after the accident happened and .... control of the situation.
6 You shouldn't .... an accusation like that if you don't have any evidence!

Vocabulary and Use of English ▶ CB pp.124–125

1 Phrasal verbs with *off*

Complete the sentences below with a phrasal verb from the box in the correct form. Use the definitions in *italics* to help you.

take off   drop off   tell off   let off   put off

1 The boy had never broken the law before, so the judge .... him .... (= *didn't punish him*)
2 Can we .... our meeting .... (= *postpone*) until this afternoon?
3 A policeman gave me a lift home and .... me .... (= *left me*) right outside my house.
4 Witnesses saw the robber's face because he .... his mask .... (= *removed*) while he was running to the get-away car.
5 Dad .... my sister .... (= *scolded*) for coming home late

take off   make off   go off   ring off wear off

6 The burglar alarm .... (= *rang*) as soon as the thieves entered the building.
7 The men robbed the bank and .... (= *escaped*) with a large amount of money and jewellery.
8 When the victim recovered from the attack he had a terrible headache but it soon .... (= *disappeared*).

9 The kidnapper phoned his victim's wife but he .... (= *put the phone down*) before the police could trace the call.
10 Sales of car alarms .... (= *have increased suddenly*) in the last ten years.

2 Lexical cloze

Read the text below and decide which answer A, B, C or D best fits each space. Use only one word in each space. There is an example at the beginning (0).

0 A amount   **B** bit   **C** deal   **D** lot

CREDIT CARD CRIME

Fraud is becoming a great (0) .*C.* more widespread these days. It is also getting harder for the police to (1) ..... it. The growing use of computers is partly to (2) ..... . Criminals who used to (3) ..... banks can now (4) ..... your credit cards and take money out of your account. Their crime may not be detected for days.

I have had (5) ..... experience of this type of fraud. It all started a year ago. A woman (6) ..... me while I was eating in a restaurant. She pushed me to the ground and (7) ..... with my wallet, my chequebook, my fifteen credit cards and my keys. I hurried (8) ..... my office and stopped my credit cards. Then I (9) ..... for my bank to close my account. It was all no (10) ..... . The woman who had taken my bag had 'become me'. (11) ..... months she went to shopping centres and used my credit card (12) ..... open new accounts.

I called the credit companies and (13) ..... them what had happened. I asked them to telephone me if anyone used my cards. But when they phoned my number, I was often at work. They heard my voice on the answer phone and so they thought (14) ..... was okay. In the end, most banks and stores were convinced that I was the sort of person who did not pay their (15) ....

1	**A** arrest	**B** charge	**C** detect	**D** find
2	**A** fault	**B** blame	**C** accuse	**D** claim
3	**A** break up	**B** break through	**C** break away	**D** break into
4	**A** rob	**B** steal	**C** burgle	**D** disuse
5	**A** a	**B** some	**C** any	**D** a few
6	**A** hijacked	**B** mugged	**C** shoplifted	**D** kidnapped
7	**A** made off	**B** made out	**C** made for	**D** made up
8	**A** at	**B** in	**C** by	**D** to
9	**A** set down	**B** set away	**C** set off	**D** set up
10	**A** value	**B** worth	**C** good	**D** hope
11	**A** During	**B** While	**C** Throughout	**D** For
12	**A** for	**B** and	**C** to	**D** by
13	**A** warned	**B** said	**C** threatened	**D** protested
14	**A** all	**B** everyone	**C** everything	**D** someone
15	**A** owings	**B** costs	**C** receipts	**D** bills

Reading: *multiple matching (summary sentences)*

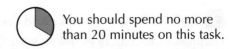

You should spend no more than 20 minutes on this task.

You are going to read a newspaper article about the fifteenth-century Italian artist, Leonardo da Vinci. Choose from the list **A–I** the sentence which best summarises each part (**1–7**) of the article. There is one extra sentence which you do not need to use. There is an example at the beginning (**0**).

A   Leonardo was working towards a final objective.

B   People at the time often copied Leonardo's ideas.

C   Leonardo seems to have been more interested in ideas than in achievements.

D   Later scientists were not able to take advantage of Leonardo's discoveries.

E   Leonardo was centuries ahead of his time.

F   Leonardo preferred to work things out for himself.

G   Leonardo preferred not to share his ideas with others.

H   Leonardo left the task of completing his life's work to others.

I   People now recognise that Leonardo was a unique person.

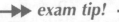 **exam strategy**   Paper 1, Part 1 ▶ CB pp.10, 54

▶▶ *exam tip!*

Work out what main point each paragraph is making, then compare your idea with the summary sentences. ◀◀

CLUES

Question:

1   Why were Leonardo's inventions so remarkable? Underline the reasons and look for the sentence that summarises the main point.

3   How many people knew about Leonardo's findings? What was the result?

5   Why did he write his notes in such a way that others could not understand them?

7   What did Leonardo care about most?

The Greatest of All Time

*A recently published book names Leonardo da Vinci as the world's first,
and possibly greatest, scientist*

0 **I**

The sixteenth-century Italian artist Leonardo da Vinci must be one of the greatest men who has ever lived. He is best remembered as a painter and a sculptor, but the extent of his abilities in other areas of knowledge is still a source of astonishment to scholars today. A recently published book describes him as the <u>world's first real scientist</u> and shows just how great his achievements really were.

1

Leonardo's imagination was so vivid, his thirst for knowledge so powerful, that he dreamt up inventions that, at the time, seemed quite impossible. He produced drawings, plans and diagrams of pieces of equipment which have come into being only in the last hundred years or so. For example, he worked out the principles for a parachute, a diving suit, contact lenses and the camera, long before the world was ready for them.

2

What drove Leonardo was his desire for information. Rather than accept what people at the time could understand and explain, he looked for a new understanding of how nature worked, gained through observation and experiments.

3

Leonardo's ideas remained largely unpublished and unknown for years after his death, however. Meanwhile, other people, ignorant of his findings, struggled to make the discoveries described in his notebooks all over again. If his ideas had been common knowledge, western science might have progressed much

faster. For example, he had sketched designs for a telescope one hundred years before Galileo came up with the same idea.

4

Although Leonardo was a very good painter, and was in great demand, he was more interested in his experiments. He wrote details of these, in no particular order, in his notebook. From time to time, he attempted to get all these notes into order. What he aimed to do eventually was to make an encyclopaedia that would contain the sum of human knowledge. This he couldn't finish, however, because he was always too busy adding to it.

5

By nature, Leonardo was a secretive man and always suspicious that others might steal his ideas. So from the beginning, his notebooks were written in

various codes, including one known as mirror writing, where the words are written in such a way that they can only be read in a mirror. Although Leonardo's discoveries destroyed many theories which existed at the time, unfortunately, few of them came to light during his lifetime.

6

And, what's more, all was nearly lost when he died in 1519. He entrusted the job of sorting out his notes to a young man called Francesco Melzi. But the task was beyond his capabilities. Melzi's son, who inherited them, was equally unable to cope and abandoned them in an attic cupboard. When the notebooks were eventually rediscovered, there were 13,000 pages remaining, containing 1,500 diagrams and anatomical drawings. Some had, however, already been lost to treasure hunters. The pages are now divided between museums and libraries all over Europe.

7

One of the great mysteries of Leonardo's character is that he started so much and finished so little. Only a handful of his paintings were completed, few of his inventions were ever made and the books he aimed to write remained unpublished. It's almost as if he was involved in so many investigations, which led him on to even more unanswered questions, that he was never able to call a halt. Towards the end of his life, he must have realised that the world of nature was too large and too complicated for even a brain like his to fully understand.

Grammar ▶ CB p.127, grammar file 22

1 *have/get something done*

1 Complete the second sentence so that it means the same as the first.

1 I must go to the hairdresser's. My hair needs cutting.
  I must go to the hairdresser's to get *my hair cut* .

2 The car needed servicing so I took it to the garage.
  I took the car to the garage to have ....

3 My computer needs to be repaired.
  I have to get ....

4 I'm going to the optician's to have an eye test tomorrow.
  I'm having my .... at the optician's tomorrow.

5 Why don't we get someone to fit better locks on our doors?
  Why don't we have .... on our doors?

6 All my CDs were stolen yesterday.
  I had .... yesterday.

2 Rewrite the following sentences using *have + object + past participle* in the correct tense.

1 The dentist took out one of my teeth yesterday.
  I *had one of my teeth taken out yesterday* .

2 The tailor is making Tom a new suit.
  Tom ....

3 The builder has built us a new swimming pool.
  We ....

4 A painter is going to decorate my room.
  I ....

5 Has the engineer repaired your computer yet?
  Has ....

6 A thief stole my jacket on the way to school.
  I ....

2 Error correction

Read the text below and look carefully at each line. Some of the lines are correct, and some have a word which should not be there. If a line is correct, put a tick (✓) in the space by the number. If a line has a word which should not be there, write the word in the space. There are two examples at the beginning (0 and 00).

PREVENTING CRIME

0	*been*	My friend, Fred, has just been had his house burgled for
00	...✓	the second time. He lives in the centre of a large city where
1	....	the crime rate is much more higher than in the village where
2	....	he grew up. I kept up telling him that he ought to do more
3	....	for to protect himself from criminals. I can't remember
4	....	the number of times I warned him of that he should get proper
5	....	locks are fitted on his doors and windows. He wouldn't listen.
6	....	Then, last year, he has had his TV and video taken. And just a
7	....	few months later, his computer was been stolen. He hadn't had
8	....	any of his possessions insured, so he couldn't get any money back.
9	....	Fred was too shocked, but the experience has forced him to change
10	....	his ways! The police have persuaded Fred to take the part in an
11	....	experiment which it could reduce the number of burglaries in the
12	....	area. Fred has agreed to have regular meetings done in his house,
13	....	to which ones he will invite his neighbours. There will be guest
14	....	speakers from the police force at each meeting. They will give advice
15	....	on having burglar alarms be fitted and tips on keeping your home secure.

Writing: *article* ▶ CB pp.50–51

1 **1 Read the exam task and answer the questions below.**

You have seen this advertisement in your college magazine:

> ### COMPETITION – FUTURE INVENTIONS
>
> Write an article for our magazine describing an invention you would like to see in the future and explaining how it would improve our lives.
>
> The best article will be published in our magazine.

Write an article for the competition in 120–180 words.

1 Who is the intended reader?
   a) the students in your college
   b) the editor of the magazine

2 Should the style be:
   a) formal/neutral?
   b) informal?

2 What do you want the article to achieve? Tick two of the following.
   a) win the competition
   b) inform the readers about inventions that are soon to be produced
   c) entertain the readers
   d) complain about the lack of equipment we have now

3 Underline the parts of the task. How many parts are there?

a) one
b) two
c) three

2 **Look at the following list of points. Choose which ones to include and put them into the paragraph plan below. Think carefully about which one would make an interesting opening paragraph.**

a) the problems that this invention will solve
b) what this invention will do
c) imaginary scene with this new invention in use
d) what this invention will look like
e) when this invention will be available
f) what kind of people will use this invention

Para. 1: introduction
(1) ....

Para. 2:
(2) ....
(3) ....

Para. 3:
the problems that this invention will solve
(4) ....

Para. 4: conclusion
(5) ....

▶▶ *exam tip!*

Remember that the first paragraph of an article needs to attract the attention of the readers and interest them enough to make them want to read on.

◀◀

3 **Now write your article. Remember to:**
● give it an interesting title
● cover both parts of the task
● divide your article into paragraphs
● write in an appropriate style

4 **Check your work.**
● Have you used a range of vocabulary and structures?
● Are the grammar and spelling correct?
● Have you used the future tenses correctly?

Progress review 3 • Units 7–10

1 Mixed tenses and modals

Put the verbs in brackets into the correct form.

A: You'll never believe what's happened. Our house (1) _has been burgled_ (burgle)!

B: Oh no! When (2) .... (it/happen?)

A: While we were at the party last night.

B: But how (3) .... (the thieves/get in)? Did they break a window, or what?

A: No, there's no broken glass anywhere. They must (4) .... (have) a key. Do you remember I (5) .... (lose) my bag last week? Someone must (6) .... (find) it and used my key to get into the house.

B: But how (7) .... (they/could/know) that you were out?

A: Well, they (8) .... (must/watch) the house for some time. They (9) .... (may/ see) us leaving the house that night in our party clothes.

B: Oh, how awful. (10) .... (they/take) much?

A: No, just £200. They (11) .... (must/only/ look) for money because they didn't take any valuables.

B: Well, we (12) .... (have/our house/burgle) last year so I know the feeling. I'm just glad none of you were hurt, though.

3 Error correction

Read the text below and look carefully at each line. Some of the lines are correct, and some have a word which should not be there. If a line is correct, put a tick (✓) in the space by the number. If the line has a word which should not be there, write the word in the space. There are two examples at the beginning (0 and 00).

2 Structural cloze

Read the text below and think of the word which best fits each space. Use only one word in each space. There is an example at the beginning (0).

THE FUTURE OF TOURISM

Tourism (0) _is_ now believed to be one of the world's biggest industries. Mass tourism began in (1) .... 1960s, when cheap air fares (2) .... first introduced by charter companies. Nowadays, a plane takes off somewhere in the world (3) .... single minute of the day! While you (4) .... reading this text, another 3,000 people will (5) .... boarding planes and flying away, either for business (6) .... for pleasure. By 2025, the number of tourists who travel abroad will (7) .... doubled. Experts predict that millions of new jobs will be created in travel and tourism (8) .... the future. In a few years' (9) .... tourists will be able (10) .... book really unconventional holidays. By 2050, for example, hotels may have (11) .... built underwater. Space hotels may (12) .... be orbiting the Earth, thanks to new technology! These hotels would no doubt be popular, (13) .... they would also be expensive. Recently, Antarctica (14) .... become a popular destination. There are no hotels at the South Pole yet. However, (15) .... has been suggested that there could be hotels all over Antarctica in the future.

A MOTOR-CYCLE RACER

0	_he_	James Haydon he is one of the best motor-cycle racers in
00	✓	the world. He began biking when he was eight. 'My dad was
1	....	interested in the motorbikes and cars and so I grew up loving
2	....	the sound and smell of engines,' he remembers himself. He kept
3	....	begging his father to buy him a motorbike until he finally got
4	....	his wish. He was thrilled with his new bike. 'I was used to
5	....	rush home from school and ride for hours. I'd ride round the
6	....	garden until it got dark!' After having seeing the speed at
7	....	which James rode, his dad decided so he would be safer
8	....	on a track. James thought that was absolutely great. He could now
9	....	ride at 90 kilometres per the hour! A few years later, his
10	....	father asked him what was he was going to do as a career.
11	....	James was a bit of worried about his answer. 'I wanted to
12	....	be a professional racer, but Dad wasn't enough impressed
13	....	by the idea!' In the end, he reached an agreement with his
14	....	dad: if he would passed all his exams, his dad would support
15	....	him. It's a decision neither of them both has ever regretted.

4 Lexical cloze

Read the text below and decide which answer A, B, C or D best fits each space. There is an example at the beginning (0).

0   **A** they   **B** who   **C** he   **D** which

HOW TO BE AN OPTIMIST

Are you the sort of person (0) _B._ always thinks the worst? Do you see a glass as half-empty instead of half-full? In other words, are you (1) .... pessimist? People who are optimists are (2) .... to be more popular than pessimists. And new (3) .... shows that optimists are healthier and live longer, too! So how can you stop (4) .... from turning into an pessimist? Here are (5) .... simple techniques which anyone can use.

First, remember that you can (6) .... choices about your moods. If you feel a bit miserable about something, try (7) .... of the good things that are happening around instead. Your bad feelings will soon wear (8) .... If you have (9) .... the train or broken something, tell yourself you don't need to go (10) .... feeling bad for days. Realise that it's just one small (11) .... Then promise yourself you're not going to think about it (12) .... more. Try to concentrate your thoughts on someone else – maybe someone you love, or (13) .... a pet. Or do something positive and practical, like (14) .... at something beautiful or smelling your favourite perfume. You could even try eating something nice – (15) .... your favourite chocolate!

---

1 **A** the	**B** one	**C** some	**D** a
2 **A** probably	**B** likely	**C** certainly	**D** surely
3 **A** research	**B** studies	**C** tests	**D** results
4 **A** one	**B** it	**C** you	**D** yourself
5 **A** some	**B** any	**C** few	**D** little
6 **A** do	**B** get	**C** make	**D** reach
7 **A** concentrating	**B** remembering	**C** reflecting	**D** thinking
8 **A** off	**B** in	**C** over	**D** down
9 **A** lost	**B** missed	**C** used	**D** forgotten
10 **A** up	**B** by	**C** off	**D** on
11 **A** accident	**B** incident	**C** happening	**D** performance
12 **A** for	**B** far	**C** any	**D** some
13 **A** also	**B** even	**C** besides	**D** yet
14 **A** listening	**B** buying	**C** watching	**D** looking
15 **A** like	**B** as	**C** such	**D** so

5 Word formation

Read the text below. Use the word given in capitals below the text to form a word that fits in the space in the text. There is an example at the beginning (0).

THE LOCH NESS MONSTER

For many centuries, people have believed in the (0) ...*existence*... of a 'Loch Ness monster'. Loch Ness is a lake in Northern Scotland. It is 39 kilometres in (1) .... It is quite narrow, but it reaches a (2) .... of 297 metres in places. Sightings of 'huge creatures' in the lake have attracted a wide (3) .... of visitors. Some of these visitors have (4) .... claimed to see 'Nessie'. They have even taken photos of the monster. However, there is a strong (5) .... that some of the photos are fakes. Scientists are (6) .... by the stories. They think it is (7) .... that monsters live in the lake. There just isn't any (8) .... They believe the shapes which visitors see on the lake may have a simple (9) .... They could be caused by the wind, by currents or even by small boats. Until someone (10) .... manages to capture her, 'Nessie' seems certain to remain a romantic legend.

---

(0) EXIST	**(6) CONVINCE**
(1) LONG	**(7) LIKE**
(2) DEEP	**(8) PROVE**
(3) VARY	**(9) EXPLAIN**
(4) OCCASION	**(10) ACTUAL**
(5) POSSIBLE	

 # The environment

Vocabulary ▶ CB Reading 1 pp.128–129

1 Word formation

Use the correct form of the word in capitals at the end of the sentence to fill the gap.

1 Researchers have established a close .... with the gorillas they are studying. **RELATION**
2 Scientists are preparing a report and will publish their .... next month. **CONCLUDE**
3 The dictionary gives a complicated .... of intelligence. **DEFINE**
4 Dolphins are .... curious animals. **NATURE**
5 There are fewer .... than you may imagine between apes and humans. **DIFFER**
6 We need stricter .... to prevent animals from being treated cruelly. **LEGISLATE**

2 Choosing the right word

Underline the correct word from the options given in *italics*.

1 *Despite/Although* dolphins are friendly, we should never forget that they are wild animals.
2 Rats *spread/sweep* disease so keep away from them.
3 The lion roared but the elephants *passed on/carried on* drinking.
4 It is *hard/hardly* to estimate how many tigers there are left in the wild.
5 Whales are among the most intelligent *populations/species* of animal in the world.
6 Some animals *pass on/carry on* their knowledge to their young.

3 Prepositional phrases

Complete the phrases in *italics* with a word from the list.

own / wild / standards / sight / captivity

1 I don't believe wild animals should be kept *in* ....
2 I don't think we can judge animals *by human* ....
3 The naturalist Jane Goodall studied apes *in the* .... in Africa.
4 We went to the safari park to see the lions but unfortunately they were nowhere *in* ....
5 The tiger cub was standing *on its* .... in the middle of the forest.

Grammar and Use of English

▶ CB pp.130–131

1 Real or unlikely conditional?

▶ grammar files 18,19

Underline the correct tense from the options given in *italics*.

1 Unless you *stop/will stop* teasing that dog, it *bites/will bite* you.
2 If you *were/would* be offered the chance to swim with dolphins, *would/did* you do it?
3 I'll go to the safari park with you as long as you *pay/will pay* for the tickets.
4 Take your camera in case you *see/will see* some animals during our visit to the safari park.
5 If my dad *didn't/wouldn't* work with animals, our family *wouldn't/didn't* know so much about them.
6 I hate zoos! I know it's impossible but I *would/will* shut all the zoos in the world if I *can/could*!
7 Mum *won't/doesn't* let my brother have a pet unless he *promises/will promise* not to bring it into the house.
8 That baby animal *never learns/will never learn* to feed itself unless its mother *teaches/will teach* it.
9 I'll go to the zoo with you as long as you *don't/won't* ask me to look at snakes!
10 You'll never lose your fear of spiders unless you *handle/will handle* them.

2 *so* or *such*? ▶ grammar files 3, 26

Read the *exam tip!* and do the exercise on page 95.

> ▶▶ *exam tip!*
>
> In **Paper 3**, **Part 3**, you may need to transform sentences with *very* and *too* into conditional sentences plus *so* and *such* in the following ways:
> 1 Anita didn't go sailing because the sea was very rough.
> **so**
> Anita would have gone sailing if the sea *hadn't been so*....... rough.
> 2 I didn't try to rescue the snake because it was too dangerous.
> **such**
> If it ..*hadn't been such a*... dangerous snake, I would have tried to rescue it.

<u>Underline</u> the correct choice from the options given in *italics*.

1 I *would go/would have gone* out if the weather hadn't been *so/such* awful.

2 If Sonya hadn't been *so/such* afraid of animals, we *might be/might have been* allowed to keep one as a pet.

3 I could *learn/have learned* to ride a horse if I hadn't been *such a/such* coward.

4 If my brother *would have known/had known* how dangerous that snake was, he wouldn't have been *so/such* brave!

5 I wouldn't have had *such/such a* wonderful birthday if Dad *hadn't taken/wouldn't have taken* us to the safari park.

3 Transformations

Complete the second sentence so that it has a similar meaning to the first sentence, using the word given. Do not change the word given. You must use between two and five words, including the word given.

1 I didn't know the sharks were harmless so I didn't swim in the sea. **swum**
If I'd known the sharks were harmless, I *would have swum* in the sea.

2 Be careful or you'll get bitten. **if**
You'll get bitten .... careful.

3 We missed feeding time at the zoo because we were very late. **so**
If we ...., we wouldn't have missed feeding time at the zoo.

4 We only visited that zoo yesterday because someone recommended it. **we**
If someone hadn't recommended that zoo, ... it yesterday.

5 The snake will only bite if you threaten it. **unless**
The snake will .... threaten it.

6 Diana is alive today because a man rescued her from the lion's cage. **be**
If a man hadn't rescued her from the lion's cage, ... today.

7 Bob was wearing protective clothes so the scorpion didn't sting him. **not**
The scorpion might have stung Bob if he .... protective clothes.

8 We didn't spend much time in the aquarium because it was a very hot day. **such**
We would have spent more time in the aquarium if it .... hot day.

9 It's a good thing you visited the safari park or you mightn't have seen the tiger cubs. **if**
You mightn't have seen the tiger cubs .... the safari park.

10 We didn't go to the wildlife park because it was too cold. **so**
We would have gone to the wildlife park if it .... cold.

4 *like* or *as*?

grammar file 3

A *like*

We use *like* + **noun/pronoun** to make a comparison:
1 *He is very **like** his father.*
2 *He drives **like** a maniac.*
3 ***Like** all teenagers, he needs his privacy.*

B *as*

We use **as**:
- **before a clause:**
  *He ran away from school **as** his brother had before.*
- **to compare two similar things or people:**
  *I'm (not) **as** tall **as** my brother.*
- **to state a person's job:**
  *She works **as** a lawyer.*
- **to describe a function:**
  *You can use this piece of wood **as** a walking stick.*
- **after certain verbs:**
  *He's a neighbour but we **regard John as** one of the family.*

Complete these sentences with *like* or *as*.

1 Tom works ...*as*......... a doctor.

2 Sarah looks .... her mother.

3 I regard my teacher .... a friend.

4 .... many small kids, my brother can be extremely annoying!

5 Here! Why don't you use my handkerchief .... a bandage.

6 He decided to study medicine .... his father.

7 This isn't the same book .... we studied last year.

8 I know we're not really related but I think of you .... one of the family.

9 I'm not .... brave .... my brother.

10 My brother swims .... a fish!

5 Auxiliary verbs

➤➤ *exam tip!*

In **Paper 3**, **Part 2** (structural cloze), you may need to fill a gap which comes before a past participle. Use the procedure below to help you find the right word.

Exam Question: The animals (1) .... fed by their keepers every morning.

Procedure:
1 The action happens 'every morning', so I need the present simple tense.
2 The sentence is passive: 'by their keepers'
3 It is also plural: 'the animals'
4 Therefore, the missing word is **are**.

◀◀

Look at the sentences below and identify the grammatical structure (e.g. active/passive, present simple/present perfect etc.). Then complete the sentences with the correct word.

1 The chimps have ..*been*...... examined by the vet.
2 By the time they finished, the scientists .... done all the research they needed to do.
3 We .... already had all these results checked twice by experts.
4 The bears were in danger of .... shot by hunters.
5 There are plans for the animals to .... rescued from the flooded areas.
6 The public .... not been told the facts yet but they will soon find them out.
7 The zoo .... opened by the President in 1920.
8 The scientific papers could have .... destroyed in the fire.

6 Structural cloze

Read the text below and think of the word which best fits each space. Use only one word in each space. There is an example at the beginning (0).

ANIMAL INTELLIGENCE

(0) ....*Until*.... recently, most scientists believed that animal behaviour (1) .... caused by evolution. However, a lot of research has (2) .... carried out into animal behaviour over the last 20 years and experts (3) .... been amazed by the results. It (4) .... becoming clear that animals possess many mental skills. These skills (5) .... highly developed in many species.

What do we know about animal intelligence? First, all animals can count. Birds (6) .... pigeons and parrots have been trained to hit a button exactly 24 times if they want to get food. Some animals are (7) .... intelligent that they can use numbers to solve problems. Second, many animals have good memories. In one experiment, monkeys (8) .... shown a banana. The banana was then hidden in a cup and the cup (9) .... placed behind a screen with other cups. In every experiment, the monkeys chose the cup where the banana (10) .... been hidden. Thirdly, animals can calculate. Birds have a mental map of the sun and stars which can (11) .... used for navigation.

Experts are now studying animal communication. We all think of monkeys (12) .... being the most intelligent animals but dolphins and whales also possess surprising skills. Scientists (13) .... been trying to analyse their calls using modern technology. Intelligent primates, such (14) .... monkeys, have developed very advanced systems of communication. Some animals have even (15) .... taught to use human sign language.

Vocabulary

▶ CB Reading 2 pp.134–135

1 Word formation

Use the correct form of the word in capitals at the end of each sentence to fill the gap.

1 You can often predict the weather by observing the .... of animals. **BEHAVE**
2 Forecasters rarely predict the weather very .... **ACCURATE**
3 The villagers lost all their .... in the floods. **POSSESS**
4 When a hurricane strikes, people get just a few hour's .... **WARN**
5 Weather conditions can be very .... **DECEIVE**
6 Tornadoes can have .... consequences. **DISASTER**

2 Choosing the right word

Underline the correct word from the options given in *italics*.

1 When the floods struck, people had to *run away/leave* their homes.
2 Yesterday we had a really *violent/extreme* storm.
3 Hurricanes *threaten/warn* people who live in tropical areas.
4 The floods were caused by the *heavy/strong* rainfall.
5 The scientists *monitored/warned* the progress of the hurricane very carefully.
6 Last year, Papua New Guinea was the *hazard/target* of a terrible storm.
7 The storm caused an enormous amount of *damage/violence*.
8 The villagers had plenty of *warning/threat* about the hurricane, so they were able to evacuate the village in time.

Vocabulary and Use of English ▶ CB pp.136–137

1 Choosing the right word

Complete the sentences below with the correct word. Use each word once only.

during for since over

1 David has been working as a scientific adviser in Borneo .... 1999.
2 Many rain forests were destroyed .... the twentieth century.
3 Biologists have not seen any examples of that species of frog .... two years.
4 Life on this planet has evolved .... millions of years.

nature country scenery wildlife

5 Peru is a .... I would really love to visit.
6 Amelia sat back on the coach and gazed at the beautiful mountain ....
7 My brother is leading a group of biologists to Borneo to study the .... there.
8 Some people agree with genetic engineering but I think scientists should stop interfering with ....

2 Lexical cloze

Read the text below and decide which answer A, B, C or D best fits each space. There is an example at the beginning (0).

0 A environs **B** place **C** environment **D** ground

HABITAT DESTRUCTION

All over the world, people are changing the face of the Earth. Wild areas are cleared for farming and to build roads and expand cities. Our factories, cars and power stations poison the (0) .C. with polluting gases and chemical (1) ..... . As well as transforming the environment, we are destroying habitats, the homes of (2) ..... plants and animals.

Living things have evolved (3) ..... millions of years. Many animals and plants can only (4) ..... in certain environments. When (5) ..... areas are destroyed, wildlife cannot always (6) ..... to the new conditions and some species may (7) ..... . Thousands of species of plants and animals face extinction because of human activities.

People can also (8) ..... from habitat destruction. When forests are (9) ..... earth is washed away, this causes crop failure and starvation. There is the future to consider, too; plants provide essential food and can also be used in medicines. If species (10) ..... extinct, their potential value will never be known.

The scale of destruction is enormous. Swamps, forests, grasslands and jungles are being cleared at an increasing (11) ..... . Half of the world's tropical rainforests have (12) ..... been destroyed. Coral reefs, called the rainforests of the ocean because they are so rich in life, are (13) ..... around the world. We must limit the (14) ..... to habitats now (15) ..... they remain a valuable resource for the future.

1	**A** rubbish	**B** nonsense	**C** remains	**D** waste
2	**A** both	**B** each	**C** every	**D** either
3	**A** over	**B** in	**C** during	**D** since
4	**A** persist	**B** survive	**C** go	**D** attend
5	**A** so	**B** this	**C** such	**D** that
6	**A** adapt	**B** use	**C** stand	**D** bear
7	**A** fade out	**B** die out	**C** give out	**D** run out
8	**A** experience	**B** feel	**C** suffer	**D** damage
9	**A** cut down	**B** pulled down	**C** put down	**D** struck down
10	**A** get	**B** die	**C** result	**D** become
11	**A** degree	**B** rate	**C** extent	**D** index
12	**A** still	**B** even	**C** already	**D** yet
13	**A** threatened	**B** violated	**C** wasted	**D** spoilt
14	**A** injury	**B** hurt	**C** damage	**D** pain
15	**A** so that	**B** in order to	**C** in case	**D** as a result

Reading: *multiple matching (questions)*

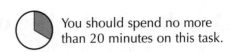

You should spend no more than 20 minutes on this task.

You are going to read an extract from a book about changing conditions in Antarctica. Answer the questions by choosing from the Sections **A–G**. The sections may be chosen more than once. There is an example at the beginning (**0**).

Which section mentions

something that has never been done before?	**0**	**C**
evidence of further developments?	**1**	
a disagreement amongst experts?	**2**	
possible negative long-term consequences of change?	**3**	
a living thing that was more plentiful previously?	**4**	
a chance to find out about the very distant past?	**5**	
the speed with which change is happening?	**6**	
how parts of Antarctica are different from each other?	**7**	
Antarctica is cleaner than other places?	**8**	
some possible explanations for what is happening?	**9**	

some positive results of the changes?	**10**
something which lasts longer as a result of the changes?	**11**
what can be learnt about the world by studying Antarctica?	**12**
seasonal variations that affect Antarctica?	**13**
wildlife that benefits from colder conditions?	**14**

▶▶ **exam strategy** Paper 1, Part 4 ▶ CB pp.46–47

┌─ ▶▶ **exam tip!** ─────────────────────────┐
Sometimes the text in **Part 4** is a continuous text rather than several short texts linked by a theme. In this case, skimming the text first can help you decide which paragraph will probably contain the information you need.
└──────────────────────────────────── ◀◀

CLUES

Question:

2 What are 'experts' in this field called? Look for this word, and for words that signal a contrast.

3 Look for a paragraph which describes both negative and long-term consequences.

6 Most of the sections include numbers. Which number is found close to a word that talks about speed?

8 What word is often used when talking about how clean or dirty the environment is?

13 What are the four seasons of the year? Look for the name of one of the seasons.

Changes affecting Antarctica

A

The Antarctic is a landmass the size of Europe and the USA put together that surrounds the South Pole. Over 99 per cent of the Antarctic is covered in a thick ice cap, in some places as thick as 4,700 m. 40 per cent of the present ice cap covers water. In addition, the continent doubles in size each winter when the surrounding seawater freezes. If we took the ice cap away, the eastern side of Antarctica would form one solid mass of mountainous land, whilst the western side would be a group of islands.

B

The Antarctic has always been good for doing scientific experiments because it is one of the few places in the world which still has a relatively unpolluted environment. What's more, by looking at the layers of ice, laid down year after year, scientists can study the history of the Earth, its seas and the atmosphere. By looking at more recent layers of ice, for example, it's possible to track, through levels of lead pollution, the spread of the motor car. And such records of how the atmosphere has changed go back over a million years in places. But recent changes in the Antarctic ice cap are of even greater interest to scientists.

C

In February 1997, the ship Arctic Sunrise, which belongs to the environmental organisation Greenpeace, became the <u>first to sail</u> around James Ross Island in the eastern Antarctic. For thousands of years, it has been impossible to do this because James Ross Island was connected to the mainland by a 200-metre thick ice shelf. But in 1995 the ice shelf called Larsen A, which runs south of James Ross Island, disintegrated and an iceberg measuring 78km by 37km broke away. Before Larsen A collapsed, it became criss-crossed with deep cracks.

Greenpeace observers have noted similar cracking in other areas of ice in the same area, which would seem to indicate that the process is continuing.

D

During the past 60 years of global warming, the Antarctic peninsula has warmed by 2.5 degrees centigrade – faster than anywhere else in the world. Some scientists think this rise is due to what is known as the greenhouse effect. That is, too much carbon dioxide gas in the atmosphere, much of it the result of fuel being burnt elsewhere on the planet, which has the effect of making the whole world too hot. Others say the warming may be localised, which means it is only happening in the Antarctic peninsula.

E

Owing to the harsh conditions, few land species of wildlife live in Antarctica. Those which do survive there have adapted to very cold conditions. They are most at risk from the changes that a warmer Antarctic is bringing. The worry now is that the effects could be more widespread. If global warming is causing the Antarctic to melt, this could cause a worldwide catastrophe. The Antarctic ice cap contains 90 per cent of the world's fresh water. If it melted completely, it would raise the sea level by more than 70 metres. Many areas of land would be flooded, including southern Britain.

F

But the news is not all bad. Rising temperatures which cause some ice to melt are beneficial to plants such as lichens and algae because as ice melts, it exposes soil where plants can live. Some species of moss are showing signs of coming back after being buried in the ice for hundreds of years. The only flowering plants in the Antarctic are the pearlwort and the Antarctic hair grass. They are now on the increase – their numbers have grown by 25 per cent in some areas.

G

Warmer temperatures can be unwelcome news for other life forms, however, particularly the penguins. The warmer weather has made it more difficult for them to bring up young, as they nest in high rocks that do not trap snow or water during the yearly ice meltdown. Because of higher temperatures there is heavier snowfall which covers nesting sites longer in the breeding season. Also, the penguins' main food is krill plankton which lives and thrives in sea covered by ice. As the ice melts, there is less krill for penguins to eat, and this has resulted in a 40 per cent decline in numbers.

Grammar ▶ CB p.139, grammar file 21

1 Reporting verbs in the passive

Complete the second sentence so that it means the same as the first.

1 It is said that the hijackers are armed.
The hijackers ...*are said to be armed*.............. .

2 It is thought that the man is innocent.
The man ....

3 It is reported that four people have been injured.
Four people ....
....

4 It is believed that the burglar entered the house through an open window.
The burglar ....
....

5 It is thought that the robbers are hiding in an empty building.
The robbers ....
....

6 It is expected that the police will arrest three people.
The police ....

2 Extra word

Two of the sentences below are correct. Tick them (✓). The other sentences contain one unnecessary word. Cross out the words.

1 The man is said to have being stolen many credit cards.

2 It is be believed that the robbers gave themselves up without a struggle.

3 A man is reported to have be helping police with their inquiries.

4 The criminals are not thought to be carrying weapons.

5 The woman is supposed to not be the leader of the gang.

6 The police are expected them to arrest the man today.

7 It is alleged that the boy punched the police officer.

8 The kidnapper it is said to have released his captives.

3 Transformations

Complete the second sentence so that it has a similar meaning to the first sentence, using the word given. Do not change the word given. You must use between two and five words, including the word given.

1 People say that floods will become more common.
said
It ...*is said that*..... floods will become more common.

2 People believe that our weather patterns are changing.
believed
Our weather patterns .... changing.

3 People fear that many species of animals are disappearing from our planet.
feared
Many species .... from our planet.

4 Scientists believe that the Earth is getting warmer.
is
It .... the Earth is getting warmer.

5 Experts think that the polar ice caps are melting.
thought
The polar ice caps .... melting.

6 People say that we are poisoning the land.
are
We .... the land.

7 People often claim that our planet is in danger.
claimed
It .... our planet is in danger.

8 Experts report that fish are dying because the sea is polluted.
reported
Fish .... because the sea is polluted.

9 Scientists believe that the rainforests contain many useful plants.
to
The rainforests .... many useful plants.

10 They expect temperatures to keep rising for some time.
are
Temperatures .... to keep rising for some time.

Writing: *report* ▶ CB pp.88–89

1 **1 Read the exam task and answer the questions below.**

> You have carried out a survey among students at your school to find out how they think your school could help the environment. Write a report for the head teacher of the school saying what you have found out and making suggestions for action to be taken by the school.
>
> Write a **report** of **120–180** words in an appropriate style.

1 Who will read the report?
   a) the students
   b) the head teacher
2 Should the style be:
   a) informal?
   b) formal?

2 Underline the parts of the task. How many parts are there?

a) one
b) two
c) three

3 What do you want the reader to do?

a) publish the report in a school magazine.
b) change the situation in the school
c) be entertained

2 **Complete the report outline opposite.**

1 Fill in the missing information at the top.

2 Write in the following headings in a logical order.

a) The present situation
b) Introduction
c) Conclusion
d) Suggested action

3 Read the following points and write them in the outline under the correct heading.

a) use less paper
b) more students should walk or cycle to school
c) you carried out a survey in the school
d) only use central heating or air conditioning when really necessary
e) many students come by car to school
f) the report is the result of a survey

To: ....
From: ....
Date: ....
Subject: ....

1 ....

2 ....

3 ....

4 ....

3 **Which of the following would be the best introduction to your report?**

1
> I asked my friends what they all thought the school should do to help the environment and this is what they said.

2
> I think that this school is not doing enough to help the environment and so I am writing a report with my suggestions.

3
> This report is the result of a survey carried out among the students at King's Hill School. The students were asked how they thought the school could do more to help the environment and what they would be prepared to do to help.

4 **Now write your report. Remember to:**

● use report format.
● cover both parts of the task.
● use headings for each section.
● use a formal style.

5 **Check your work.**

● Have you used a range of structures and vocabulary?
● Are the spelling and grammar correct?
● Have you used impersonal passive constructions correctly?

12 Careers

Vocabulary ▶ CB Reading 1 pp.140–141

1 Word formation

Use the correct form of the word in capitals at the end of each sentence to fill the gap.

1 When I left the Hall after my .... ceremony, I had no idea what to do. **GRADUATE**
2 I don't like sitting at a desk – I prefer to do work that is very .... **PRACTICE**
3 I've been in the job for two years and now I'm hoping for .... **PROMOTE**
4 What do you .... me to do after I leave school? **ADVICE**
5 I have a job that offers me a lot of .... **RESPONSIBLE**
6 After I finish school next year, I'm going to do .... work in India. **VOLUNTEER**

2 Phrasal verbs

Complete the sentences below with a phrasal verb from the box in the corrrect form. Use the definitions in brackets to help you.

go on	take on	track down	build up	find out

1 The company is expanding and needs to .... (= *employ*) new staff.
2 What was .... (= *happening*) in the office last week?
3 I've just managed to .... (= *find with difficulty*) a friend that I haven't seen for years.
4 I was surprised to .... (= *discover*) that my friend wanted to be a teacher.
5 If she wants to start her own business, she'll need to .... (= *gradually increase*) a list of contacts.

3 Verb + noun collocations

Complete the collocations below with a verb from the list. The noun is in *italics* is to help you.

become / give / join / get / spend / start

1 His brother wants to .... *the army.*
2 My friend is hoping to .... *a place* at medical school.
3 We're going to .... *time* getting to know the area before we start work.
4 Could you .... *me some advice* about what I should do next year?
5 I'm going to .... *a lawyer* when I leave school.
6 My sister wants to .... *her own business.*

Grammar and Use of English ▶ CB pp.142–143

1 Wishes ▶ grammar file 20

Put the verbs in brackets into the correct form.

1 I'd like to buy a car but I'm too young to drive. I wish I ...*were*..... (be) older.
2 I can't afford a holiday. If only the boss .... (give) me a pay rise!
3 My teacher wishes he .... (earn) more money!
4 I've told you that twice already. I wish you .... (pay) attention.
5 I wish I .... (speak) English more fluently.
6 If only I .... (not/fall over) when I went in for my interview!
7 I wish I .... (not/have to) leave school this year but I do.
8 Do you ever wish you .... (be) rich?
9 I didn't hear what the boss said. I wish I .... (listen) more carefully.
10 I wish the bus .... (come). I'm going to be late for work again.

2 I'd rather, I'd prefer

grammar file 20

We use **would prefer** in the following ways:

- **would prefer + to-infinitive + (rather) than + infinitive without to**:
  I'd prefer to earn a living (rather) than stay at school.
- **would prefer you/he/they (not) + to-infinitive**:
  I'd prefer you not to smoke in the office.
- **would prefer it if you/he/they + past simple**:
  I'd prefer it if you didn't shout all the time!

Underline the correct options from the choices given in *italics*.

1 It's time I *was leaving/will leave*.
2 I'd rather you *not to tell/didn't tell* anyone about this.
3 I'd prefer you *not to come/not coming* tonight. I've got so much to do!
4 The manager said he'd prefer *you would telephone/it if you telephoned* tomorrow.
5 It's high time he *change/changed* his job.
6 We'd prefer *staying/to stay* late tonight rather than tomorrow.
7 He'd rather *study/to study* medicine than be a lawyer.
8 Don't you think it's about time you *do/did* some work?

3 Transformations

Complete the second sentence so that it has a similar meaning to the first sentence, using the word given. Do not change the word given. You must use between two and five words, including the word given.

1 I regret not being able to speak more languages.
   wish
   I wish .... *I could speak* .... more languages.
2 I'd prefer you not to ring me at work.
   rather
   I .... ring me at work.
3 My brother regrets taking that job.
   wishes
   My brother .... that job.
4 I'm sorry I didn't go to college.
   only
   If .... to college!
5 I think you should go to bed now!
   time
   It .... to bed!
6 I prefer studying to going out to work.
   rather
   I .... out to work.
7 I'm very bad at Maths. **so**
   I wish .... at maths.
8 I'd like my boss to stop shouting at me.
   only
   If .... shout at me.
9 They should be leaving for the airport now.
   time
   It .... for the airport!
10 I'm sorry you're not working here next week.
   wish
   I .... here next week.

4 Auxiliary verbs

 exam tip!

In **Paper 3**, **Part 1**, pay special attention to the words **has, had** and **having** in front of gaps. These words may be followed by:
- **a past participle**: *I have **done** it.* (perfect tense)
- **an infinitive + to**: *I had **to go out**.* (modal verb expressing necessity)
- **a noun**: *I had **breakfast**.*
- **a pronoun**: *I'm fed up with long hair so I'm having **it** cut tomorrow.*
- **an article**: *I've just had **a** fight with my brother.*
- **an adverb**: *I have **never** been to Paris.*

Complete these sentences with one word.

1 We will have .... interview the candidates today.
2 I have .... my *curriculum vitae* typed out by a secretary.
3 His work has .... checked by the teacher.
4 We have .... looking forward to going to the safari park for ages.
5 Does he have .... good college degree?
6 She has .... wanted to be an actor.

5 Structural cloze

Read the text below and think of the word that best fits each space. Use only one word in each space. There is an example at the beginning (0).

TAKING A YEAR OUT

Imagine the scene. You have (0) ....*been*.... sitting indoors for weeks revising for exams, while everyone else has been having (1) .... great time. At this moment, you are dreaming (2) .... a different life. You imagine yourself on a beach (3) .... some remote part of the world. Does all this seem (4) .... a dream? Well, that dream could come true!

Remember that travel can (5) .... educational. You learn a (6) .... deal about life – and yourself – when you spend time abroad. Nowadays, many young people have (7) .... year off before they start university. During this year they learn new skills (8) .... explore their interests. But it is important to spend the time wisely. Remember that you will have (9) .... come back and start studying again when the year has (10) .... Nobody will be impressed if you have (11) .... your time lying in bed, listening to hip-hop music and watching TV!

You could go to Nepal and teach English. Some people have even (12) .... employed as yak farmers in the Andes! This may sound romantic but you (13) .... to think about money, too. In (14) .... end, you may have to take (15) .... job you can, or maybe two.

Vocabulary ▶ CB Reading 2 pp.146–147

1 Prepositions

<u>Underline</u> the correct preposition from the options given in *italics*.

1 What qualities are necessary *to/for* someone to be a great musician?
2 Eric Clapton is one of the most famous rock guitarists *of/in* the world.
3 Make sure you don't take *on/up* too much work or your studies will suffer.
4 The children are rehearsing *with/for* a concert.
5 My teacher keeps an eye *on/at* how I'm progressing.
6 I could play the piano when I was younger but now I'm *out of/away from* practice.

2 Word formation

Use the correct form of the word in capitals at the end of each sentence to fill the gap.

1 My best friend is a fantastic .... **MUSIC**
2 Her talent has been .... praised in the local newspaper. **HIGH**
3 She likes playing rock and .... music. **CLASSIC**
4 One day she hopes to get a job as a violin .... with a big orchestra. **SOLO**
5 She's really .... so she often enters talent contests. **COMPETE**
6 She's just heard that the President will be at her next ....! **PERFORM**

3 Adjectives

1 Match the adjectives in column A with their meanings in column B.

A	B
1 challenging	a) deserves the time you spend on it
2 dull	b) difficult but exciting
3 exhausting	c) dirty and untidy
4 mature	d) fully grown and developed
5 scruffy	e) uninteresting
6 thrilling	f) unpaid/not compulsory
7 voluntary	g) extremely exciting
8 worthwhile	h) extremely tiring

2 Complete the sentences below with an appropriate adjective from column A.

1 I decided to become a nurse in spite of the long hours and low pay because I wanted to do something really ....
2 You shouldn't go for an interview in such .... clothes.
3 The party was really .... I don't know when I've been so bored!
4 Instead of going straight into paid employment, Richard is going to do .... work helping people in Africa.
5 Stella's job is so .... that she has to go to bed as soon as she gets home every night!
6 Emma's parents think she is very .... for her age but I think she's rather childish.
7 The course I've just finished was very .... – I thought I'd never keep up with the other students but I managed it in the end.
8 I've had some .... news. I've been offered a fantastic job on television!

4 Compound adjectives

! *Using hyphens*

We usually put a hyphen between compound adjectives before a noun e.g.:
*My father wears really **old-fashioned clothes**.*

Complete the sentences below with compound adjectives formed by matching a word in column A with a word in column B.

A	B
1 bad	a) time
2 first	b) looking
3 full	c) handed
4 good	d) tempered
5 left	e) class

1 Katya is a *first-class* pianist. She's won lots of prizes.
2 When I leave school, I'll need a .... job.
3 He's a really .... guy; he's tanned and fit and he's got wonderful eyes!
4 I'm .... so I need a specially made guitar.
5 My music teacher is really .... He's always shouting at us.

Vocabulary and Use of English

▶ CB pp.148–149

1 Word formation

Read the information in the box. Then fill the gaps in the following sentences 1–6 with an appropriate adverb from the box.

Adverbs

Some adverbs, such as **hard**, **late**, **wide**, have two forms, depending on the meaning.

- **hard/hardly**
1 *Don't work too **hard**!*
  (= too much)
2 *I can **hardly** hear you.*
  (= I can only hear you with difficulty)

- **late/lately**
1 *Don't be **late**!*
  (= unpunctual)
2 *Tom hasn't been in the office **lately**.* (= recently)

- **wide/widely**
1 *Open the door **wide**, please.*
  (= the greatest distance possible)
2 *My brother travels **widely** in his job.*
  (= to a lot of places)

1 I've been studying really .... recently.
2 My sister has been working abroad ....
3 The dentist told me to open my mouth ....
4 I've been so busy I've .... had time to think.
5 We mustn't be .... for college.
6 I have travelled .... since I took this job.

2 Word formation

Read the text below. Use the word given in capitals below the text to form a word that fits in the space in the text. There is an example at the beginning (0).

A DAY IN THE LIFE OF ...

As director of a large holiday company, Chris has a great deal of (0) *responsibility*. . He starts the day at 8 a.m. every Monday with a meeting to discuss customer (1) .... He and his team study the customer questionnaires they have received very (2) .... and review the results together. They also discuss health and (3) .... issues. Chris spends about half his time travelling round the world, checking how much (4) .... there is from other companies. He finds that meeting customers is a (5) .... part of his job. He goes round all the company's hotels and listens (6) .... to all his customers' suggestions. While he is listening, he notes down all the (7) .... people make. Most people are (8) .... satisfied with the company. Looking back to his education, Chris values his time at university. He says that it taught him (9) .... and confidence. All in all, he says, it was an extremely (10) .... experience.

(0) RESPONSIBLE	(6) ATTENTIVE
(1) SATISFY	(7) RECOMMEND
(2) CARE	(8) HIGH
(3) SAFE	(9) INDEPENDENT
(4) COMPETE	(10) MEMORY
(5) VALUE	

Reading: *gapped text*

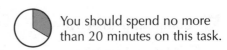

You should spend no more than 20 minutes on this task.

You are going to read a magazine article about a disc jockey. Seven paragraphs have been removed from the article. Choose from the paragraphs **A-H** the one which best fits each gap. There is one extra paragraph which you do not need to use. There is an example at the beginning (**0**).

The life of a DJ

Imagine a full-time job where you travel the world playing records at dance clubs in return for large amounts of money. For British DJ Paul Bryant, this is a reality.

You could say that the British DJ Paul Bryant is at the top of his profession. Paul, who started off his career at the age of sixteen, recently added to his long list of successes when he was voted 'Best DJ of the Year'. It's his third major award in recent years.

0	H

By the time he was seventeen, Paul not only had his own music programme on a small radio station, but he was also appearing every Saturday night at another top London club. Before long, he was making a name for himself as a pioneer of an exciting new type of dance music called 'house music'. It developed into one of the biggest dance crazes of the early 1990s.

1	

As if all that travelling wasn't enough, Paul is still to be seen at some of the biggest dance clubs in the UK. He's also the resident Friday night DJ at his father's club, where his career began.

2	

Although Paul sometimes misses the 'good old days', when things were simpler, he is positive about the growth of these various types of dance music. 'I think going to dance clubs is a lot of fun. It's a great way for young people to let off steam,' he says. 'There's a lot of choice and variety, different types of music especially, and that's good.'

3	

Paul recalls: 'A lot of those old tracks bring back fantastic memories of going out dancing with my friends, hearing great records at clubs and then going out and trying to buy them somewhere.'

4	

And that's just what Paul has always done. For Paul, popular culture is not something which stands still. He can see where the music scene is going, and he keeps one step ahead. That's why the music he plays as a DJ, and the records he produces, will always be popular.

5	

With the reputation Paul has managed to build, you might think the record company would leave the choice of tracks to him, but that's not always the case. 'With a record like this, they spend a lot of money on the publicity campaign, so they've got to make sure that the music's going to appeal to a lot of people,' Paul explains.

6	

But does doing it this way mean that Paul is more interested in producing a million seller than in including his own favourites? 'Things generally become popular because they're good,' he insists. And let's face it, if anyone can spot a winner on the dance scene, it's Paul Bryant.

A When Paul started out there, there wasn't much variety in terms of the actual music that DJs played. Today, it's completely different, and new styles of music with weird and wonderful names are springing up all the time.

B Paul's newest CD is a good example of this. It's a compilation album featuring the type of music he is currently playing, and is aimed at the widest possible audience.

C As the dance club scene continues to grow, and clubs try to cater for a wider audience, some of the older clubbers feel that dance music has become too commercial. They say that the music has dropped in quality.

D Paul, on the other hand, has never doubted his own judgement. He continues to play what he likes.

E And he admits that he still likes to go out to a club and hear those old records himself every now and then. But he's also quick to point out: 'You've got to move with the times.'

F They put forward the songs they think should be on there. He goes through the list, taking them off here and putting them back on there, adding his own selection only occasionally.

G Over thirteen years later, Paul commands respect amongst DJs and fans all over the world. Now 29, Paul regularly works in clubs in the USA, Japan, South America and Australia.

H Born and bred in London, Paul really grew up in the music scene. His father owns the club where he played some of his first dance record mixes as a teenager.

 *exam strategy*   Paper 1, Part 3 ▶ CB p.34

▶▶ *exam tip!*

Don't choose your answers too quickly. If you have difficulty finding an answer, this may mean you have already used the correct answer for another question, so you should go back and check.

◀◀

CLUES

Question:

1 The paragraph after this question mentions travelling. In which extract A–H is travelling introduced?

4 In the paragraph after this question it says 'popular culture is not something which stands still'. In which extract does Paul say something similar?

5 The paragraph after this question talks about a record. In which extract is this idea introduced?

Grammar ▶ CB p.151

1 Linking expressions

Contrast
To introduce a contrast or an
opposing argument, we can use:

- *despite/in spite of/in spite of the fact that*:
  *She got the job in spite of/despite **her nerves**/being nervous/**the fact that** she was nervous.*
- *However/Nevertheless + comma*:
  *He loved school. **However**,/ **Nevertheless**, he had to leave.*
- *On the other hand*:
  *The salary is good but **on the other hand** the hours are long.*

Underline the correct linking words
from the options given in *italics*.

1 Tom's going to leave, *even if/in spite of* the boss offers him a higher salary.
2 He couldn't save the business from disaster *despite/in spite* all his efforts.
3 She is now managing director *although/however* she only joined the company a while ago.
4 *While/However* I don't want to leave my job, I do want to travel round the world.
5 It would be great to study medicine but *on the other hand/despite* I really enjoy drama.
6 My parents want me to stay at school. *But/However*, I'd prefer to get a job.
7 I'd like to be a lawyer *however/even though* it means studying a lot.
8 My friends think I'd be a fantastic actor *but/nevertheless* I don't agree.

2 Linking expressions

Addition, cause and result
To add information, we can use:

- *as well as/in addition to + ing* form/noun:
  As well as/In addition to working in the factory, he is a DJ at weekends.
- *Furthermore/Moreover/What's more + comma*:
  *The boss congratulated me. **What's more**, he offered me a rise.*
- *too* at the end of a clause:
  *I enjoy swimming, and I like riding, **too***

**Complete the sentences below with linking words from the list.
You won't need to use all the words.**

as / as well as / because / because of / furthermore / too / so / in spite of the fact that

1 The factory is closing .... the lack of orders.
2 The boss praised us for our work. ...., he said we could all take a day off!
3 I'm not feeling well .... I'm not going to work today.
4 .... he invented a new machine, he didn't make much money.
5 .... offering me promotion, the company are sending me to the USA for a year.

3 Structural cloze

Read the text below and think of the word which best fits each space. Use only one word in each space. There is an example at the beginning (0).

A JOB ABROAD

When I left school I wasn't sure what to do (0) ......*so*...... I decided to go abroad. (1) ...., there was just one small problem. I had (2) .... experience of travel – and I didn't have any money, (3) .... ! I didn't speak any foreign languages, (4) .... did I have any qualifications. Then a friend suggested we work our way around the world. What a great idea! I told my parents. I thought they would be delighted (5) .... they were furious! They said that it was not only impractical, but it was dangerous (6) .... (7) .... first I argued with them, but in the (8) ...., I saw that they were right. We were too young for such a big adventure, (9) ...., of course, we thought we were very grown up!

So, my friend and I sat down and thought again. We were determined to find jobs abroad, in (10) .... of the difficulties. We wrote to lots of organisations, but we were turned down (11) .... of our ages. (12) ...., we took jobs as *au pairs*! I had five children to look after. As (13) .... as being young, they were naughty! But even (14) .... it was hard work, I loved it. I was really sad to leave (15) .... the end of my time with them.

Writing: *discursive composition*

▶ **CB Reading 2 pp.138–139**

1 **Read the exam task and answer the questions below.**

> Your class has recently had a discussion on part-time work for young people and your English teacher has asked you to write a composition, giving your opinions on the following statement:
>
> *It is a good idea for young people to do part-time work while they are studying.*
>
> Write a **composition** in **120–180** words in an appropriate style.

1 Who is going to read your composition?
  a) your class   b) your teacher
2 Should the style be:
  a) informal?   b) neutral?

2 What are the three ways you could write this composition? Fill in the gaps below:

1 argue in ...*favour*... of the idea
2 argue .... the idea
3 give .... sides of the argument

2 **Look at the following points. Tick (✓) the arguments <u>for</u> the statements and put a cross (✗) next to the arguments <u>against</u> the statement in the exam task.**

a) Students have less time to spend studying.
b) They can gain valuable experience.
c) Employers use them as cheap labour.
d) They have more money to spend.
e) They do not watch so much television.
f) They have no time to enjoy themselves.

 *exam tip!*

It is better to take just a few ideas, e.g. two or three for each side of the argument, and develop them well. If you try to include too many different ideas, your composition will be more like a list than an argument.

3 **Using some of the ideas in Exercise 2 or your own ideas, make a paragraph plan for your composition. Remember to:**

- decide at the beginning which way you are going to organise your composition.
- plan at least four paragraphs.
- think of examples to illustrate your arguments.
- organise your ideas.
- plan your introduction and conclusion.

Para. 1: Introduction

....

Para. 2: Points for students working

....

....

....

Para. 3: Points against students working
Students have less time to spend studying.

....

....

Para. 4: Conclusion

....

....

4 **Now write your composition. Remember to:**

- state your opinion clearly.
- use appropriate linking words.
- use a neutral style.

5 **Check your work.**

- Is your opinion clear?
- Have you used a range of vocabulary and structures?
- Are the grammar and spelling correct?

Progress check 3

Grammar

1 Hypothetical meaning
Put the verbs in brackets into the correct form.

1 I wish my brother .... (close) the door when he goes out.
2 It's time we .... (buy) a new washing machine.
3 I wish I .... (can) afford to buy a bigger flat.
4 I wish I .... (take) my teacher's advice last year.
5 Would you rather .... (work) in the summer or go on holiday?
6 I'd rather you .... (pay) me in cash than by cheque.
7 Come on, it's time .... (go)! We'll miss the bus.
8 If only I .... (try) a bit harder, I might have won the gold medal.

2 Conditionals
<u>Underline</u> the correct conditional form from the options given in *italics*.

1 I might have got the job if I *would have/had* prepared myself better for the interview.
2 If I *will discover/discover* who the thief was, I will let you know.
3 If you had waited a little longer last night, you *would see/would have seen* the animals come to the water to drink.
4 What *would you do/will you do* if you were bitten by a snake?
5 If there *is/were* a hurricane, we would not be well prepared.
6 If Tom *were/had been* here last night, he would have known what to do.
7 If I have a cold, I usually *will take/take* extra vitamins.
8 I know that it would be better if I *would saved/saved* my pocket money.

3 Tense forms
Put the verbs in brackets into the correct form.

1 By the end of this century thousands of species of animals .... (die) out.
2 Can you buy some wood because I .... (put) up some bookshelves this afternoon.
3 I'm sure that soon people .... (live) under the sea.
4 Sam .... (think) of changing his job soon.
5 This time tomorrow we .... (lie) on a beach a thousand kilometres away.
6 I .... (wait) for the bus when it started to pour with rain.
7 Tom .... (work) on the same book for five years now.
8 When we met, I knew I .... (see) John somewhere before.
9 After waiting for half an hour, Sue .... (leave) a message and went home.
10 I don't think they .... (arrive) before 9 o'clock because they didn't leave until 6.

4 Modal verbs
Complete the sentences with a suitable modal verb in the correct form.

1 Sue is away on holiday. You .... seen her here yesterday.
2 We expected them to arrive an hour ago. I'm sure they .... forgotten about the meeting.
3 Anything's possible. Ian .... decided to visit someone on his way home.
4 After hours of shouting, at last they .... to attract somebody's attention.
5 You .... keep your seatbelt fastened during the flight.
6 Do you think you .... to come to the party next Saturday?
7 You .... shouted at her like that, she's really upset now.
8 Joe was pleased when he realised he .... pay for tickets for the match because they were free for students.

5 Extra word
Some of the sentences below are correct. Tick them (✓). The other sentences contain one unnecessary word. Cross out the words.

1 Joe can't afford to have someone his car repaired.
2 It would be a good idea to have installed a burglar alarm.
3 My mother had painted my room for me last week.
4 After the Browns had had their house extended, the children left home.
5 The old trains really need to replacing with faster, more modern ones.
6 The roof really needs to be been repaired before the winter.

6 The passive
Complete the second sentence so that it has a similar meaning to the first sentence.

1 It is expected that water levels will rise considerably over the next 50 years.
Water levels ....
2 Dolphins are believed to be able to communicate quite sophisticated messages.
It is ....
3 People think that a cure for the common cold will be found in the near future.
It is ....
4 It is said that the crime rate is increasing.
The crime rate ....
....

Vocabulary

7 Word formation

1 Complete the table.

	Noun	Verb	Adjective
1	*information*	inform	....
2	....	....	fascinating
3	....	understand	....
			....
4	....	....	discovered
5	solution	....	....
6	....	reduce	....
7	thought	....	....

2 Use the correct form of the word in capitals at the end of each sentence to fill the gap.

1 There has recently been a .... in the number of people using their cars to get to work. **REDUCE**

2 I found the lecture about the environment very .... **INFORM**

3 Can you all tell me your .... on the proposal to build a new theatre in the town centre? **THINK**

4 Tom was .... very concerned when he heard that he may lose his job. **UNDERSTAND**

5 Nobody knew where the ship had sunk and it lay .... for several centuries. **DISCOVER**

8 Prepositions

Fill the gaps with a suitable preposition.

1 Boredom amongst young people can lead .... an increase in crime.

2 Improvements in technology will result .... more leisure time for working people.

3 Television and computers can prevent young people .... studying.

4 Advertisements encourage people to spend money .... things that they do not need.

5 The view over the mountains reminds me .... my home village.

6 What is the best way .... getting promoted?

7 Try and make use .... every opportunity to practise speaking English.

8 Will you please help me to fill .... this application form?

9 Who is responsible .... the food at the party?

10 Are you good .... learning languages?

9 Choosing the right word

Underline the correct word from the options given in *italics*.

1 Join the video club to see all the *last/latest* films at reduced prices.

2 It can be difficult to get to *asleep/sleep* if you work very late.

3 The train is *due/time* to arrive in five minutes.

4 Computer systems need to be *updated/dated* every couple of years.

5 In the *conclusion/end* we decided to go home early.

6 To *sum/end* up, I think that it would be a good idea to ban the use of private cars.

7 *Firstly/At first* the weather isn't good enough for a picnic.

8 Alan has been out of *work/job* for almost six years.

10 Linking words

Complete the sentences with a linking word from the box.

although	despite	in spite	whereas	even if

1 .... extensive research, it has not been possible to find a cure for many diseases.

2 My parents prefer to stay in good hotels .... of the cost.

3 I think we should go on the trip .... it rains.

4 .... he's got the right qualifications, he really has no experience of the job.

5 Working from home is very convenient, ... if you travel to work you can waste several hours a day.

Answer Key

1 Entertainment

Vocabulary ▶ p.4

1 1 drawings 2 director 3 extremely
   4 organisation 5 specially 6 length

2 1 audiences 2 script 3 crew 4 set
   5 scenery 6 theme

3 1 make 2 play 3 achieve 4 hire 5 pay
   6 form

Grammar and Use of English ▶ p.4

1 1 do you think 2 's/is reading
   3 don't understand, flies, goes, loves, finds, decides,
   doesn't like 4 'm/am thinking 5 's/is training
   6 sounds 7 's/is always talking 8 do you feel
   9 's/is appearing 10 'm/am working

2 1 <u>often</u> play 2 I have <u>never</u> been … 3 … don't
   <u>usually</u> have enough time … 4 … my sister has
   <u>always</u>
   wanted … 5 We <u>rarely</u> go … but we go to the
   cinema <u>now and again</u>. 6 They don't <u>usually</u>
   show … 7 I have <u>never</u> seen …
   8 My brother is <u>always</u> complaining …

3 1 is coming 2 we're going, we'll miss, I'll video
   3 Shall I ask 4 I'll go 5 I'll get
   6 are showing, I'll stay

4 1 is going to rain 2 're/are going to visit
   3 'll/will do 4 'm/am going to be
   5 Are you going to see 6 'll/will drive

5 1 is bound to win 2 is about to start 3 is likely
   to play 4 are going to meet 5 am always losing
   things 6 is due to start at 7 are unlikely to finish
   8 are bound to enjoy 9 probably won't be/will
   probably not be 10 will certainly get seats

Vocabulary ▶ p.6

1 1 illustrations 2 management 3 collection
   4 thought 5 discussion 6 choice 7 exhibition
   8 intention

2 1 join 2 take 3 offer 4 keep 5 solve

Vocabulary and Use of English ▶ p.6

1 1 getting on with 2 got over 3 got away with
   4 get out of it 5 getting at 6 get down to

2 1 Although 2 in spite of 3 However 4 While
   5 too 6 also 7 so 8 as 9 Neither
   10 either 11 Nevertheless 12 Despite

3 1 C 2 D 3 B 4 A 5 A 6 A 7 C 8 C
   9 A 10 B 11 D 12 A 13 B 14 D 15 D

Reading ▶ p.8

1 E 2 D 3 H 4 C 5 G 6 F 7 A

Grammar ▶ p.10

1 1 have always been 2 acted 3 has just opened
   4 did you watch, gave 5 have never had
   6 have ever read

2 1 have been rehearsing 2 has already starred
   3 has just closed 4 have been waiting
   5 has just won 6 have been filming

3 1 phoned 2 ✓ 3 … has been filming …
   4 We queued … 5 … he has ever done … 6 ✓

4 1 has been working 2 did you start training
   3 has (only) just started 4 have been touring for
   5 have been rehearsing for 6 haven't been to
   7 I have ever 8 first time Tom has (ever)
   9 hasn't been used for 10 has been important
   since

Writing ▶ p.11

1.1 1 c) 2 b)

1.2 1 ✓ 2 ? 3 ✓ 4 ?

2.1 2 b) 3 b) 4 a) 5 a) 6 b) 7 b) 8 a) 9 a)
   10 b)

2.2 a) 3 b) 10 c) 9 d) 2 e) 1 f) 7

3 Suggested paragraph breaks after:
   … to make a career in the theatre.
   … give me the opportunity to do so.

2 Challenges

Vocabulary ▶ p.12

1 1 incredibly 2 leadership 3 strength
   4 unimaginable 5 psychological 6 optimism

2 1 horror 2 hope 3 spirits 4 danger
   5 display

3 1 from 2 about 3 from 4 to

Grammar and Use of English ▶ p.12

1 1 was having 2 saw 3 were planning
   4 were looking 5 sighed 6 looked 7 was
   typing 8 were ringing 9 did 10 thought 11
   didn't want 12 was still thinking 13 came
   14 gave 15 decided

2 1 had already climbed, suddenly started
2 saw, ran 3 reached, had disappeared

3 1 had explored 2 had left 3 had been climbing
4 had eaten

4 1 had only been diving 2 were exploring
3 were waiting 4 had been lying

5 1 I had been lying 2 jumped up 3 had caught
4 had been trying 5 was drowning 6 jumped
7 dived 8 had been struggling 9 swam
10 had gathered

6 1 while they were travelling 2 she had never
been to 3 had been flying for 4 were still
climbing 5 while he was working in 6 since he
did 7 as soon as he arrived 8 had never flown
9 went to France when 10 since they travelled

7 1 were 2 have 3 had 4 had 5 were
6 was 7 have 8 has

8 1 were 2 were 3 were 4 did 5 had
6 was 7 had 8 were 9 had 10 were
11 were 12 were 13 did 14 was 15 had

Vocabulary ▶ p.14

1.1 1 e) 2 g) 3 a) 4 h) 5 b) 6 c) 7 f) 8 d)

1.2 1 squeezed 2 glided 3 dangling 4 emerged
5 waded 6 strolled 7 collapsed 8 clambered

2 1 have a go at 2 acquire a new skill
3 Pay attention 4 make friends 5 take turns
6 lost my nerve

Vocabulary and Use of English ▶ p.15

1 1 irresponsible 2 hopeless 3 sensible
4 impatient 5 enthusiastic 6 rainy
7 incapable 8 courageous

2.1 1 adjective 2 noun 3 noun 4 adjective
5 adjective 6 adjective 7 noun 8 adjective
9 noun 10 adjective

2.2 1 energetic 2 activities 3 instructors
4 unqualified 5 safety 6 unnecessary
7 death 8 attractive 9 reality 10 frightening

Reading ▶ p.16

1 C 2 D 3 B 4 A 5 C 6 D 7 A

Grammar ▶ p.18

1 1 Where can I go bungee-jumping?
2 How much does it cost for students?
3 Is there a long queue?
4 How early do you start in the morning?
5 What is the minimum age?
6 Is it necessary to wear a helmet?

2 1 Can you tell me where I can hire equipment?
2 I would like to know how much a hang-gliding
lesson costs.
3 Where can I find the instructor?
4 ✓
5 I would be grateful if you could tell me what the
price is.
6 Must I wear special clothes?
7 ✓
8 How many people will there be on the
expedition?

3 1 b) 2 a) 3 b) 4 a) 5 a)

4 1 be grateful if you could 2 tell me when I should
3 wonder if I need 4 to know if there is
5 if I will get 6 to ask if/whether you have
7 to ask if it would 8 you let me know when
9 tell me how to get/I get

Writing ▶ p.19

1.1 1 c) 2 c)

1.2 b) ask how much experience necessary
e) ask which area in the Himalayas
g) ask how much it costs h) ask what minimum
age is/about minimum age

1.3 1 say I'm interested 2 ask how much experience
necessary 3 ask about accommodation
4 ask how much it costs/about cost 5 hearing
from you 6 sincerely

2 **Sample answer:**

Dear Ms. Blake,

I am writing in response to your advertisement for
someone to join you on your trip to the
Himalayas. I am very interested but first I wonder
if you could give me some more information.

You mentioned the autumn but I would like to know
the exact dates as I am not free until the beginning
of October. I would also like to know if you have a
minimum age. Although I am only 18, I have been
climbing for six years and I have climbed some of
the most difficult climbs in the Alps. Would that be
enough experience?

I would also be grateful if you could let me know
which area in the Himalayas you are planning to go
to and explain what you mean by difficult
conditions. What kind of accommodation will you
be staying in and how much will the whole trip
cost?

The trip sounds very exciting and it's a wonderful
opportunity. I hope very much that I will be able
to join you. I look forward to hearing from you.

Yours sincerely,

Progress review 1 ▶ p.20

1 1 appear 2 are sitting 3 are holding 4 look
5 think 6 don't seem 7 is shouting 8 are
turning 9 imagine 10 are carrying

2 1 are giving 2 are they coming 3 'll/will have
4 Shall I phone 5 'll/will have to 6 open
7 are you doing 8 are going 9 is getting
10 are going to live

3 1 John was sitting in the park last Saturday afternoon.
2 He had gone to bed late the night before so he
was feeling/felt tired now. 3 He closed his eyes
and relaxed. 4 They were playing his favourite
song on the radio and so he turned up the volume.
5 He had been sitting like that for about ten minutes
when he suddenly heard a noise. 6 He looked up.
A small boy was standing in front of him. It looked
as if he had been/was crying. 7 John looked
round. 8 There was nobody else around. The child
had probably run away from his parents and got lost.
9 He spoke to the child and discovered he had been
wandering around the park for some time. 10 John
took the child to the nearest police station where his
parents were waiting anxiously.

4.1 1 I have to 2 did the producer tell you
3 had forgotten 4 I had to 5 Has the producer
arrived 6 has just finished

4.2 1 you first became 2 've/have wanted/have been
wanting 3 do they feel 4 didn't tell 5 left
6 are you planning 7 you could 8 have never
spoken 9 are you going to do 10 'm/am going
to do

5 1 courageous 2 hopeless 3 excitement
4 famous 5 illustrations

6 1 A 2 A 3 C 4 B 5 B 6 C 7 B 8 D 9 C
10 D

3 Education

Vocabulary ▶ p.22

1 1 agency 2 invitation 3 unbelievably
4 ambition 5 architectural 6 specialise
7 qualifications 8 Technology

2 1 lucky break 2 talent scout 3 screen test
4 bright lights 5 spare time 6 late nights

Grammar and Use of English ▶ p.22

1 1 to do 2 going, seeing, leaving 3 to do
4 helping 5 coming 6 doing 7 wear, to learn
8 use

2 1 dancing, to phone 2 locking, to turn on
3 driving, to get 4 playing, to win
5 to interrupt, checking 6 to start, pushing

3 1 of him to ring 2 of her to drive 3 of Jake to
jump 4 of her to give up 5 of my friend to win
6 of you to walk 7 of our teacher to give us
8 of you to lose

4 1 on passing 2 for not writing 3 to sitting
4 to working 5 to meeting 6 on swimming
7 at playing 8 of lying

5 1 are not interested in 2 didn't mean to worry
3 wouldn't/didn't let them go 4 don't mind
studying 5 spent ages getting to 6 'd/would
rather not go 7 not go out 8 hard for him to get
9 remind me to post

Vocabulary ▶ p.24

1.1 2 employment 3 solution, soluble
4 occupation, occupied 5 fascination, fascinating,
fascinated 6 education, educational, educated

1.2 1 advertising 2 successful 3 unemployment
4 supporters 5 possibility 6 solution

2 1 by 2 at 3 by 4 from 5 for 6 at

3 1 settle in 2 work out 3 set up 4 draw up
5 break into

4 1 attends 2 invest 3 postpone 4 solve
5 missed 6 spend 7 persuaded 6 harmed

Vocabulary and Use of English ▶ p.25

1 1 tutor 2 professor 3 lecturer 4 fail 5 take
6 pass 7 place 8 room 9 space
10 certificate 11 degree 12 licence

2 1 C 2 D 3 D 4 B 5 D 6 A 7 B 8 D 9 A
10 C 11 D 12 A 13 C 14 D 15 C

Reading ▶ p.26

1 C 2 D 3 B 4 H 5 A 6 F 7 E

Grammar ▶ p.28

1 1 is 2 is 3 do 4 weren't 5 shines 6 save, won't

2 1 will 2 will 3 would 4 don't 5 ✓ 6 do
7 will 8 ✓

3 1 I were you I wouldn't 2 provided (that) you pay
3 as/so long as you work 4 if I could afford 5
unless you hurry 6 it weren't 7 I had more
money, I 8 were you I wouldn't 9 unless Paul
goes 10 in case it rains

Writing ▶ p.29

1.1 1 b) 2 b)

1.2 c) length of course? d) accommodation?
e) excursions?

1.3 Reasons are needed for:
the number of hours; the length of course

2 1 b)   2 a)   3 b)

3 **Sample answer**:

Dear Sam,

Thanks for your letter. It's great that you want to go on an English course – I'm sure you'll find it improves your English a lot.

I think you would have a better time at the London school because there isn't much going on at night in Southend. As for the hours and the length of the course, it is better to do 15 hours a week and stay for a month. If you do 25 hours a week, you won't have enough time to go sightseeing and enjoy yourself. Also in just 2 weeks you won't get used to speaking English and start making progress.

About accommodation, when I was there I stayed in a hostel for the independence but I did not practise English enough. I would advise you to stay with a family.

You asked about the excursions. They are expensive – it's cheaper to go on your own. But you should go on the city tour because it helps you to work out where everything is.

Let me know if you need any more information.

Best wishes,

4 Places

Vocabulary ▶ p.30

1 1 peaceful   2 fortunate   3 freedom   4 incredible
5 pollution   6 cultural   7 tremendously
8 decision

2 1 drawbacks   2 according   3 longs   4 suburbs
5 runs   6 relationship   7 Despite   8 going up

3 1 budget   2 means   3 mess   4 control
5 whole

Grammar and Use of English ▶ p.30

1 1 better   2 more dangerous   3 friendlier
4 farther/further   5 ugliest   6 happier
7 least hard-working   8 fewer   9 less polluted
10 craziest

2.1 1 The guide spoke much too quickly.
2 I'm not tired enough to go to bed.
3 That river is too dangerous for people to swim in.

4 The music was too slow for us to dance to.
5 Make sure you have enough money to pay for your ticket.
6 The shelf was too high for me to reach.
7 The roads were too narrow for us to drive along.
8 He didn't explain clearly enough for me to understand.

2.2 1 The coffee was too hot to drink.
2 I'm not strong enough to lift that suitcase.
3 It was raining so the bench was too wet to sit on.
4 He was too tired to go to the party.
5 It's too late to go out.
6 The streets aren't wide enough to drive along.

3 1 is much more polluted than   2 get, the more
exciting   3 too hot (for us) to   4 the cheapest
flight to   5 isn't/is not as cheap as   6 tallest I have
ever   7 not old enough to   8 too quickly for me to

4 1 I feel hungry.
2 The disco appears closed/seems to be closed.
3 She looks like a fashion model.
4 The people in this city don't seem to understand English.
5 It looks as if it's going to rain this afternoon./
It looks like rain this afternoon.
6 Mum doesn't look as if she's very pleased with us today!

5 1 enough   2 like   3 ✓   4 them   5 more   6 ✓
7 be   8 ✓   9 much   10 ✓   11 most   12 than
13 for   14 more   15 than

Vocabulary ▶ p.32

1 1 about   2 about   3 of   4 ✓   5 about   6 at
7 of   8 ✓

2 1 from   2 of   3 along   4 in   5 in   6 in
7 around   8 to   9 at   10 to

Vocabulary and Use of English ▶ p.33

1.1 1 impolite   2 disagree   3 unfasten   4 illogical
5 dislike   6 irrelevant   7 disapprove
8 disappearance

1.2 1 ✓   2 disbelief   3 ✓   4 unforgivable   5 illegal
6 ✓   7 irresponsibly   8 misbehaved

2.1 1 adjective   2 adjective   3 adjective   4 noun
5 verb   6 adjective   7 adjective   8 noun
9 verb   10 verb

2.2 1 national   2 impossible   3 unavoidable
4 involvement   5 enable   6 traditional
7 uncomplicated   8 enjoyment   9 misbehave
10 encourage

Reading ▶ p.34

1 C   2 B   3 D   4 C   5 B   6 A   7 B   8 C   9 A
10 D   11 A   12 D   13 C   14 D

Grammar ▶ p.36

1 1 Majorca is an island <u>where many people spend their holidays</u>.
2 There is a disco near the hotel <u>which/that plays fantastic music</u>.
3 The bedroom <u>which/that I share with my brother</u> overlooks the sea.
4 I've got some photographs of the house <u>(which/that) we stayed in/where we stayed</u> on our holidays.
5 Our town is full of hotels <u>which/that are empty in the winter</u>.
6 There is an island off the coast <u>where only 50 people live</u>.
7 I have just visited some friends <u>whose house is near the sea</u>.
8 The house <u>where my aunt lives</u> is absolutely huge.

2 1 him 2 it 3 what 4 it 5 at 6 ✓ 7 they 8 ✓

3 1 which 2 It 3 who 4 where 5 lots/plenty 6 to 7 also 8 of 9 whose 10 well 11 of 12 for 13 when 14 why 15 who

Writing ▶ p.37

1 1 b) 2 b) or c) 3 b)

2.1 a), b), e)

2.2 Suggested ideas:
What people do: dance; give present;
What you like: atmosphere; buying new clothes

2.3 Suggested plan:
Paragraph 1: introduction – description of what happens
Paragraph 2: the importance of the festival, what people do
Paragraph 3: How people prepare for the festival
Paragraph 4: Conclusion: – what I like about it

3.1 b)

3.2 b)

4 Sample answer:

The place to be this summer

Summer is always a time for having fun, maybe by going to the cinema and especially to the open air cinema. This is what the International Film Festival in Karlovy Vary in the Czech Republic is all about.

You can watch up to 30 films a day, if you can take it. There is an enormous range of film genres, from old silent films to modern adventure films, from scientific documentaries to alternative art films.

It is made especially enjoyable by the huge programme of other activities taking place all around this beautiful spa, which is stylishly decorated for the occasion. Fashion shows give you an idea for your new look and there are concerts where you can enjoy rock, country or orchestral music.

So, there is no point in staying at home and missing this international event with its marvellous atmosphere and the opportunity to meet and talk to the famous names of the film world. This festival is definitely not about being bored. Come to Karlovy Vary!

Progress check 1 ▶ p.38

Grammar

1 1 have never been 2 did 3 has performed 4 played 5 did you leave

2 1 wanted 2 had been walking 3 hadn't revised 4 had been raining/had rained 5 had ever seen 6 was studying

3 1 going 2 to buy 3 staying 4 to find 5 telling 6 to study 7 paying 8 using 9 to try 10 decorating

4 1 allow 2 made 3 want 4 let

5 1 than 2 the 3 most 4 like 5 as 6 the 7 better 8 as 9 least 10 more

6 1 much 2 enough 3 ✓ 4 too 5 of 6 ✓

7 1 Valerie, who teaches us French, has just won an award.
2 The old lady, whose husband was a famous explorer, lives at the top of the hill.
3 Do you remember that summer when we used to play by the river on the way home from school?
4 I have found my own special place, where I can escape from all the noise at home.
5 Have you seen the latest production of *Hamlet*, which is on at the National Theatre?
6 The book that I would recommend for your revision is quite cheap.

Vocabulary

8

	Noun	Verb	Adjective
1	origin	originate	original
2	enjoyment	enjoy	enjoyable
3	criticism	criticise	critical
4	ability	enable	able
5	explanation	explain	explanatory
6	equipment	equip	equipped
7	life	live	lively
8	excitement	excite	exciting
			excited

9 1 excitement 2 enjoyable 3 criticism
4 explanation 5 ability 6 equipment

10 1 in 2 in 3 at 4 of 5 on 6 on 7 in
8 from

11 1 do 2 spectators 3 up 4 making
5 interested 6 frozen 7 out 8 easily
9 capable 10 mark

5 Lifestyles

Vocabulary ▶ p.40

1 1 exhibition 2 equipment 3 personal
4 visitors 5 similarly 6 inspiration

2 1 latest 2 stocks 3 match 4 tips
5 autographs 6 queues

3 1 stock 2 offer 3 fact 4 display 5 roof

Grammar and Use of English ▶ p.40

1 1 have to 2 ought to 3 mustn't 4 managed
5 needn't have bought 6 didn't need to
7 ought not 8 must

2 1 to buy 2 ✓ 3 to 4 had to 5 ✓ 6 to buy
7 mustn't 8 not to buy

3 1 weren't able to 2 weren't allowed to take
3 didn't need to 4 managed to find 5 needn't
have reminded 6 will be able to 7 must not
waste 8 can't drive without 9 may not leave
10 had to go

4 1 need 2 had 3 be 4 ✓ 5 have 6 to
7 ✓ 8 be 9 manage 10 ✓ 11 be 12 ✓
13 must 14 had 15 to

Vocabulary ▶ p.42

1 1 stressful 2 possessions 3 inexpensive
4 informal 5 temptation 6 carefully

2 1 spent 2 scattered 3 take 4 lead 5 last
6 mood 7 made 8 wardrobe 9 suits
10 cope

Vocabulary and Use of English ▶ p.42

1.1 1 added up 2 try on 3 saved up 4 take off,
put on 5 show off

1.2 1 throw out 2 make out 3 work out 4 set out
5 wear out

2 1 voyage 2 travel 3 trip 4 journey 5 think
6 mind 7 mean 8 intend 9 experiment
10 experience 11 test 12 research

3 1 D 2 A 3 B 4 C 5 A 6 C 7 C 8 D 9 A
10 D 11 D 12 B 13 B 14 D 15 B

Reading ▶ p.44

1 B 2 A 3 C 4 B 5 D 6 C 7 A

Grammar ▶ p.46

1.1 1 she had been to the shops the day before
2 I (should) take the jacket back to the store the
next day
3 the jeans would be cheaper the following week
4 they were expecting new stock in later that
morning
5 the store would be open the next day
6 I could pay later … I had to pay then

2 1 to 2 me 3 ✓ 4 previous/before 5 did
6 to 7 ✓ 8 on

3 1 complained the sweater had shrunk 2 whether
he could have 3 enquired whether/if the shop
opened 4 me why I had not 5 suggested that
Peter should 6 protested she hadn't touched
7 when she had bought 8 she was going to/would
9 (that) he had to buy 10 if I would like

Writing ▶ p.46

1 1 a) 2 a) 3 b)

2 c) many stalls closed early d) not all goods
local – some imported f) some performers didn't
arrive, e.g. (examples will vary)

3 1 I bought … 2 I ate/had … 3 Many stalls
closed early. 4 Not all goods local – some goods
imported. 5 Several performers didn't come:
(example).

4 Sample answer:

Dear Sir or Madam,

I am writing to comment on the article about the craft fair in your paper last week. I would like to point out that some of the facts were not correct.

It is true that there were some very good things about the fair. For example, the food was delicious. I had a very tasty home-made soup. Also the goods for sale were excellent quality and I found a beautiful pair of hand-made earrings for my mother's birthday.

However, it is not true that all the goods were locally made; some were imported from other countries. Your article also said that the fair was very well organised. In fact there were several problems. For example, many of the stalls closed as early as 4 p.m. and some of the entertainers didn't arrive. The fact that there was no magician was a particular disappointment for the children. The fair was very well supported but that meant that it was too crowded because there was not enough space for so many people.

I hope the organisers will try to avoid these problems next year.

Yours faithfully,

6 Family life

Vocabulary ▶ p.48

1 1 adolescence 2 rebellious 3 privacy
4 terribly 5 anxiety 6 patience 7 unfortunately
8 arguments

2 1 in 2 at 3 from 4 in 5 on 6 on

Grammar and Use of English ▶ p.48

1.1 1 to keep 2 that we apologise 3 me to go out
4 me to enter 5 that we go 6 reading 7 me to go 8 not to tell

1.2 1 B 2 A 3 B 4 B 5 A

2 1 Franco not to leave his 2 denied breaking
3 that George phone his 4 realised (that) he had forgotten 5 told her to be 6 reminded Stella to buy 7 suggested going to 8 apologised for losing 9 admitted breaking 10 offered (to give) Paul

3.1 1 set off 2 grows up 3 broken down
4 showing off 5 lie down

3.2 1 let ... down 2 back ... up 3 told .... off
4 brought ... up 5 pick ... up

3.3 1 going out with 2 run out of 3 put up with
4 get on with 5 going on at

4 1 down 2 of 3 up 4 on 5 by 6 ✓
7 by 8 ✓ 9 to 10 it 11 up 12 off
13 out 14 it 15 ✓

Vocabulary ▶ p.50

1 1 explorer 2 boring 3 incredibly 4 acting
5 unemployment 6 proud 7 successful
8 comforting

2 1 at 2 on 3 under 4 on 5 in 6 in 7 at
8 from

Vocabulary and Use of English ▶ p.51

1 1 f) 2 d) 3 e) 4 b) 5 c) 6 a)

2 1 While 2 As 3 during 4 if 5 so 6 as
7 Despite 8 Although 9 In spite 10 even
11 otherwise 12 even though

3 1 C 2 D 3 B 4 B 5 C 6 B 7 D 8 A 9 D
10 D 11 D 12 C 13 D 14 B 15 A

Reading ▶ p.52

1 B 2 D 3 A 4 A 5 C 6 C 7 B 8 A 9 D
10 D 11 C 12 B 13 A 14 C

Grammar ▶ p.54

1 1 get 2 live 3 used 4 used to 5 use
6 always used to 7 got 8 use

2 1 d) 2 f) 3 b) 4 a) 5 e) 6 c)

3 1 be 2 to 3 would 4 were 5 being/playing,
6 ride 7 never 8 get 9 sitting 10 shout
11 used 12 was 13 am 14 got 15 will

Writing ▶ p.55

2.1 Suggested order: b), d), c), a)

2.2 1 b) 2 b) 3 d) 4 d) 5 d) 6 c) 7 a)

3 1

4 Sample answer:

After twenty years

As she rang the doorbell, Susan felt a mixture of fear and excitement. She had been waiting for this moment for a long time yet she doubted if it was the right decision to go there and to ring the doorbell. She hoped no one would come to open the door.

Susan was only four when she saw her father for the last time. Her mother had never talked about him and about the reason why he had left them. Susan had seen a few pictures of her father but she had never known what to feel towards him.

Susan didn't know what to expect from this meeting. It was no wonder that she couldn't imagine her father as she hadn't seen him for more than twenty years. She was just thinking she should leave when the door opened.

Susan couldn't say anything but there was no need. A few seconds later they were clasped in each other's arms and they stayed there for several long minutes.

Progress review 2 ▶ p.56

1 1 leaving 2 going 3 having to 4 to escape
5 to go 6 stay 7 telling 8 fighting 9 going
10 shout/shouting 11 going 12 to swim

2 1 were 2 would stay 3 stay 4 will get
5 bring 6 would not be able 7 didn't have
8 wouldn't spend 9 were 10 had 11 would
prefer 12 will send 13 like 14 came
15 would take

3 1 who 2 could 3 me 4 more 5 which
6 going 7 them 8 later 9 had 10 lets
11 as 12 to 13 unless 14 more 15 where

4 1 B 2 D 3 A 4 D 5 C 6 C 7 A 8 C 9 B
10 C

5 1 colourful 2 Unlike 3 variety 4 unbelievably
5 possessions 6 valuable 7 temptation
8 possibly 9 arguments 10 enjoyment

7 Fitness

Vocabulary ▶ p.58

1 1 moody 2 irrational 3 boredom 4 anxious
5 unhelpful 6 failure 7 excitement 8 silence

2 1 tears 2 pressure 3 proportion 4 ordinary

3 1 about 2 with 3 with 4 from 5 with

Grammar and Use of English ▶ p.58

1 1 is believed 2 had been cancelled 3 have been
told 4 will be held 5 is being interviewed
6 were announced 7 will be opened 8 is closed
9 was being taken 10 were given

2 1 to buy 2 servicing 3 testing 4 to go
5 washing 6 to study 7 cutting 8 to get
9 to have 10 lengthening

3 1 to be given 2 be taught 3 not be put
4 have been told to 5 have been offered 6 to
have been warned 7 should have been discussed
8 be offered

4 1 is expected to 2 are being bought (by teenagers)
3 has to be changed 4 is being treated 5 needs
fixing 6 is going to/will be published 7 was
made to pay 8 was being discussed by 9 wasn't
allowed to go 10 should have been done

5 1 who 2 who 3 which 4 which /that
5 whom 6 whose

6 1 who 2 to 3 needs/has 4 can/will/may
5 few 6 are 7 is 8 should/must
9 that/ which 10 that/which 11 are 12 done
13 not 14 been 15 will

Vocabulary ▶ p.60

1.1 1 d) 2 f) 3 e) 4 a) 5 b) 6 c)

1.2 1 goggles 2 punchbag 3 whistle 4 flippers
5 helmet

2 1 do 2 spends 3 Take 4 pay 5 make
6 goes

Vocabulary and Use of English ▶ p.61

1.2

VERB	ADJECTIVE	NOUN
1 develop	developing developed	development
2 xxxxxxxxxxxx	innocent	innocence
3 disappoint	disappointed disappointing	disappointment
4 survive	surviving	survival
5 empty	empty	emptiness
6 excite	exciting excited	excitement
7 xxxx	polite	politeness
8 persuade	persuasive	persuasion

2 1 depth 2 strength 3 width 4 length

3 1 nineteenth 2 proposal 3 enthusiastic
4 conference 5 excitement 6 planning
7 decision 8 highly 9 payment 10 competitor

Reading ▶ p.62

1 G   2 E   3 D   4 F   5 C   6 B

Grammar ▶ p.64

1.1 1 b)   2 c)   3 d)   4 e)   5 a)

1.2 1 I went to the pool for a swim.
2 She ran so as not to be late home.
3 We arrived early in order to avoid the queues.
4 They went to the gym to do some aerobics.
5 We trained hard so that we would be ready for the race.
6 He phoned his parents so that they would not be worried.

2 1 There   2 It   3 There   4 It   5 There   6 There
7 There   8 It

3 1 in order to get
2 as not to get
3 is necessary to arrive early
4 (in order) to/so as to/to impress
5 so as to get
6 in order to win
7 so as not to disappoint/in order not to disappoint
8 for a walk
9 in order to make
10 was difficult to find

Writing ▶ p.65

1.1 1 a)   2 b)

1.2 b) and d)

1.3 d)

2 Paragraph 1: **b)**
Paragraph 2: **b)**
Paragraph 3: **c)**
Paragraph 4: **a)**

3 Sample answer:

Dear Alex,

Thanks very much for your letter. You asked me to describe my modern jazz dance lessons, which I recently took part in for the first time.

Every lesson starts with a warm-up and different exercises, which can sometimes be very hard. You stretch your muscles to prevent injuries and build up stronger muscles too. After the warm-up, our teacher always introduces us to the figures and steps we have to dance. For a better understanding, we dance these steps without music.

To dance for three hours without any break sounds very difficult but if you enjoy dancing, you'll get used to it. I really love jazz dance because you can become very fit while having fun. Although I have only spent a short time dancing, I feel much healthier and even a little thinner now.

I know that you did some ballet in your younger days, so maybe you would like to come along and take part.

Please write back soon,

Yours,

8 Travel

Vocabulary ▶ p.66

1 1 diving   2 behaviour   3 exceptionally
4 improvement   5 knowledge   6 relaxing

2 1 in   2 on   3 in   4 in   5 for   6 at   7 on
8 into

3 1 spend   2 take   3 make   4 learn

Grammar and Use of English ▶ p.66

1.1

Countable nouns	Uncountable nouns
tourist	weather
vacancy	fun
trip	advice
ticket	information
person	peace
suitcase	traffic
restaurant	luggage
problem	help
	shopping

1.2 1 some 2 any 3 some 4 a 5 some
6 some/any 7 an 8 any 9 any 10 a

2 1 so 2 such 3 such an 4 so 5 such
6 such 7 so 8 such

3 1 little 2 a little 3 many 4 a few 5 little
6 many 7 a little 8 a few

4 1 Either 2 Both 3 nor 4 each 5 plenty of
6 any 7 Neither 8 either

5 1 the 2 a 3 the 4 ✓ 5 the 6 a 7 ✓
8 the

6 1 the 2 little 3 the 4 a 5 of 6 ✓
7 hardly 8 ✓ 9 a 10 ✓ 11 many 12 of
13 ✓ 14 so 15 the

Vocabulary ▶ p.68

1 1 heat 2 protection 3 happily 4 ignorance
5 tourism 6 inhabitants

2 1 sandy 2 natural 3 working 4 family-run
5 high 6 protected

Vocabulary and Use of English ▶ p.69

1 1 in 2 at 3 about 4 to 5 on 6 for

2 1 for 2 in 3 of 4 to/from 5 for/about
6 with 7 with/about 8 about/of

3 1 with 2 for 3 in 4 on 5 from 6 for
7 on/about 8 on

4 1 A 2 B 3 C 4 B 5 A 6 D 7 C 8 D 9 C
10 B 11 C 12 A 13 B 14 D 15 B

Reading ▶ p.70

1 G 2 A 3 F 4 B 5 E 6 D

Grammar ▶ p.72

1 1 must all work together to save our planet
2 shouldn't have left rubbish about
3 ought to do what the guide tells them
4 needn't have cut down all those trees
5 shouldn't hunt the animals
6 they don't need to build a new road
7 could have stopped tourists coming to our island
(but we didn't)
8 should be doing more to protect wildlife

2 1 be 2 have 3 to 4 been 5 not
6 have/need 7 have 8 be

3 1 had to close 2 needn't have walked 3 be
doing 4 ought not to have been 5 don't have to
6 must regulate 7 should not have picked
8 need to protect 9 have done more 10 didn't
need to cut

Writing ▶ p.73

1.1 1 a) 2 a) and c) 3 b)

1.2 describing the tourist attraction; suggestions for how
the day might be organised

1.3 a), d) and g)

2.1 2

2.2 1 e), f) 2 b), c) and h) 3 i)

2.3 c)

3 **Sample answer:**

To: The School Principal

From: Maria Schmidt

Date: 3 April

Subject: Class visit – the Wren Route

Introduction
My proposal is that we go on a guided walk to
investigate the architecture of Sir Christopher
Wren in the City of London. Many students know
about St Paul's Cathedral, but they do not realise
that Wren also built other monuments.

Practical matters
There are organised one-hour walks which pass
ten of Wren's churches and seven church towers.
The meeting point is in front of St Paul's
Cathedral every odd hour from 11a.m. to 5p.m.
The cost is only £1 per person. They will take a
maximum of 30 people on each walk, so it might
be necessary to book a special walk for our
school.

The day
The best way to organise the day would be to
take the Underground train to St Paul's, do the
walk and then have a picnic lunch by the river.

Conclusion
This would be a good opportunity to learn about
the history of the buildings and the life of
Sir Christopher Wren and also to hear some new
stories, gossip and myths about London and the
people who used to live there.

Progress check 2 ▶ p.74

Grammar

1 1 don't have to 2 have to 3 shouldn't 4 were
able to 5 should 6 shouldn't 7 needn't have
got up 8 ought to

2 1 much 2 a 3 ✓ 4 an 5 ✓ 6 a 7 of 8 ✓

3 1 had   2 previous   3 whether/if   4 where
5 would   6 they   7 that   8 was   9 next
10 should

4 1 have known   2 hurt   3 had been   4 was
waiting   5 had ever travelled   6 have been
looking   7 finish/have finished   8 did you spend
9 will visit   10 are you planning to do

5 1 were you, I'd   2 too much exercise, you might
3 didn't go swimming three times a week, he
wouldn't   4 don't hurry up, you won't   5 need
something/anything, don't hesitate

6 1 get used to   2 used to/would   3 get used to
4 used to   5 am used to/have got used to

7 1 to   2 for   3 in   4 as   5 order

Vocabulary ▶ p.68

8.1

	Noun	Verb	Adjective	Negative adjective
1	*replacement*	replace	*replaceable*	*irreplaceable*
2	excess	*exceed*	*excessive*	xxxxxx
3	*attraction*	attract	*attractive*	*unattractive*
4	*competition*	*compete*	competitive	*uncompetitive*
5	*restoration*	restore	xxxxxx	xxxxxx
6	advice	*advise*	advisable	*inadvisable*
7	*supervision/ supervisor*	*supervise*	supervised	*unsupervised*
8	benefit	*benefit*	*beneficial*	xxxxxx

8.2 1 restoration   2 irreplaceable   3 advisable
4 unsupervised   5 excessive

9 1 specially   2 injury   3 straight   4 benefits
5 journey   6 change   7 cure   8 despite
9 aches   10 meet

10 1 held up   2 drove off   3 put up with   4 face
up to   5 check in

9 Discoveries

Vocabulary ▶ p.76

1 1 existence   2 proof   3 unsuitable   4 unlikely
5 explanation   6 increasingly

2 1 of   2 from   3 for   4 with   5 of   6 on   7 of
8 for

Grammar and Use of English ▶ p.76

1 1 can't   2 can't, must   3 might   4 can't be
5 can   6 must   7 may   8 can't   9 must
10 can't

2 1 couldn't have seen, must have been dreaming
2 ✓   3 can't have been listening   4 ✓
5 can't be trying   6 must have lost
7 must have imagined it   8 can't have gone

3 1 must be   2 might not be telling   3 must have
been   4 can't have gone   5 must have been
working   6 can't be staying   7 can't have been
captured   8 could have been   9 may be watching
10 might have visited us

4 1 he   2 ✓   3 it   4 her   5 it   6 ✓   7 they
8 we   9 it   10 he

5 1 they   2 been   3 ✓   4 them   5 he   6 ✓
7 it   8 ✓   9 had   10 ✓   11 to   12 ✓
13 been   14 might   15 had

Vocabulary ▶ p.78

1 1 settlement   2 came across   3 picked up
4 looked like   5 turned out   6 sewn   7 depth
8 preserved

2 1 wild   2 stone-age   3 heated   4 freezing
5 latest

Vocabulary and Use of English ▶ p.79

1.1 1 generosity   2 honesty   3 creativity
4 necessity   5 ability   6 scarcity   7 invisibility
8 possibility

1.2 1 majority   2 nationality   3 publicity   4 variety
5 responsibility   6 jealousy   7 probability
8 opportunity   9 similarities   10 suitability

2 1 scientists   2 completely   3 intelligence
4 unable   5 assumption   6 surprisingly
7 communication   8 behaviour   9 arrival
10 possibility

Reading ▶ p.80

1 A   2 C   3 C   4 D   5 B   6 B

Grammar ▶ p.82

1 1 Having missed   2 being   3 Knowing
4 Seeing/Having seen   5 Shaking   6 having seen
7 being   8 knowing

2 1 it   2 when   3 ✓   4 him   5 ✓   6 who
7 as   8 because   9 in   10 ✓   11 up   12 over
13 which   14 like   15 ✓

Writing ▶ p.83

1 1 b)   2 b)   3 b)

2.1 Points for: a), c), d)
Points against: b), e), f)

2.2 1 a)–d)   2 a)–d)   3 a)–d)   4 e)   5 e), f)

3.1 1 b),   2 a),   2 d),   4 c)
Note: a) and d) could be in either order.

3.2 This paragraph plan gives both sides of the argument.

4 **Sample answer:**

Preserving historical buildings

Why should we preserve historical buildings? There are many points to consider and a decision about where to invest our money is essential.

Firstly, old buildings help us to learn about past cultures, people and their lives, for example the ancient Greek and Roman palaces and temples. Another reason for keeping these buildings is that many of them were beautifully designed and constructed. Every day millions of tourists admire the architecture of previous centuries. Everyone wants to see attractive places and to enjoy unique experiences.

However, there are also some disadvantages. Old buildings are expensive to maintain and it is difficult to protect them from vandalism. Some of them are ugly, in bad condition and even dangerous, for example disused factories from industries that have died out or moved to better accommodation.

I think that as long as people travel around the world to see the most attractive and famous buildings, it is important to keep at least the best. The worst should be knocked down to make space for more modern, practical buildings.

---

10 Technology

Vocabulary ▶ p.84

1 1 confident 2 useful 3 unfashionable 4 vanity 5 relatively 6 sticky 7 advice 8 information

2 1 accessory 2 stares 3 gadgets 4 inventions 5 frowned

3 1 end 2 market 3 Internet 4 e-mail 5 whole 6 date

Grammar and Use of English ▶ p.84

1 1 will be flying 2 won't use 3 will be taking off 4 Will you be eating 5 'll/will give 6 will be going/are going, Will you buy 7 will be taking 8 Will you still be studying

2 1 will have put 2 will you have finished 3 will have been working 4 will have left 5 Will your group already have finished 6 will just have got 7 will have been typing 8 will have taken over

3 1 ✓ 2 himself 3 ✓ 4 myself 5 ✓ 6 myself 7 ✓ 8 yourself 9 ✓ 10 ✓

4 1 has 2 have 3 ✓ 4 be 5 ✓ 6 up 7 already 8 ✓ 9 done 10 that 11 ✓ 12 as 13 still 14 also 15 that

Vocabulary ▶ p.86

1 1 thefts 2 robberies 3 accuracy 4 variety 5 security 6 reliable 7 freedom 8 physically

2 1 in 2 against 3 for 4 between 5 of 6 for 7 on 8 between

3 1 taken 2 make 3 take 4 made 5 took 6 make

Vocabulary and Use of English ▶ p.87

1 1 let … off 2 put … off 3 dropped … off 4 took … off 5 told … off 6 went off 7 made off 8 wore off 9 rang off 10 have taken off

2 1 C 2 B 3 D 4 B 5 B 6 B 7 A 8 D 9 C 10 C 11 D 12 C 13 A 14 C 15 D

Reading ▶ p.88

1 E 2 F 3 D 4 A 5 G 6 H 7 C

Grammar ▶ p.90

1.1 1 my hair cut 2 it repaired 3 my computer repaired 4 eyes tested 5 better locks fitted 6 all my CDs stolen

1.2 1 had one of my teeth taken out yesterday.
2 is having a new suit made.
3 have had a new swimming pool built.
4 am going to have my room decorated.
5 your computer been repaired yet?
6 had my jacket stolen on the way to school.

2 1 more 2 up 3 for 4 of 5 are 6 has 7 been 8 ✓ 9 too 10 the 11 it 12 done 13 ones 14 ✓ 15 be

Writing ▶ p.91

1.1 1 a) 2 b)

1.2 a) and c)

1.3 b)

2 Suggested order:
Paragraph 1: c)
Paragraph 2: d) and b)
Paragraph 3: f)
Paragraph 4: e)

3 Sample answer:

> **A world without petrol?**
>
> Imagine a world with no traffic pollution, where there is no concern about rising fuel prices or shortages of fuel. I would like to see the invention of a car that will allow all this to happen.
>
> What would be special about this car? Although it would look like a normal car, it would have new equipment inside. Everybody would see the difference when the engine started. Actually, it would have no engine at all. Instead, this car would have solar batteries.
>
> Obviously this car would have a lot of advantages. It would be economical and it would not pollute the atmosphere. The only thing it would need to keep it going would be light – even a very small source of light would be enough.
>
> It is not unusual to use solar energy, but nobody has succeeded in making a car with batteries that run on this type of energy. To make it work, it will be necessary to produce these cars cheaply and also to attract public interest in buying them. I hope that this will happen very soon.

Progress review 3 ▶ p.92

1 1 has been burgled 2 did it happen 3 did the thieves get in 4 have had 5 lost 6 have found 7 could they have known 8 must have been watching 9 may have seen 10 Did they take 11 must only have been looking 12 had our house burgled

2 1 the 2 were 3 every 4 are 5 be 6 or 7 have 8 in 9 time 10 to 11 been 12 even/already 13 but 14 has 15 it

3 1 the 2 himself 3 ✓ 4 was 5 ✓ 6 having 7 so 8 ✓ 9 the 10 was 11 of 12 enough 13 ✓ 14 would 15 both

4 1 D 2 B 3 A 4 D 5 A 6 D 7 D 8 A 9 B 10 D 11 B 12 C 13 B 14 D 15 A

5 1 length 2 depth 3 variety 4 occasionally 5 possibility 6 unconvinced 7 unlikely 8 proof 9 explanation 10 actually

11 The environment

Vocabulary ▶ p.94

1 1 relationship 2 conclusions 3 definition 4 naturally 5 differences 6 legislation

2 1 Although 2 spread 3 carried on 4 hard 5 species 6 pass on

3 1 captivity 2 standards 3 wild 4 sight 5 own

Grammar and Use of English ▶ p.94

1 1 stop, will bite 2 were, would 3 pay 4 see 5 didn't, wouldn't 6 would, could 7 won't, promises 8 will never learn, teaches 9 don't 10 handle

2 1 would have gone, so 2 so, might have been 3 have learned, such a 4 had known, so 5 such a, hadn't taken

3 1 would have swum 2 if you're not 3 hadn't been so late 4 we wouldn't have visited 5 not bite you unless you 6 Diana wouldn't be alive 7 hadn't been wearing 8 hadn't been such a 9 if you hadn't visited 10 hadn't been so

4 1 as 2 like 3 as 4 Like 5 as 6 like 7 as 8 as 9 as, as 10 like

5 1 been 2 had 3 have 4 being 5 be 6 have/has 7 was 8 been

6 1 was 2 been 3 have 4 is 5 are 6 like 7 so 8 were 9 was 10 had 11 be 12 as 13 have 14 as 15 been

Vocabulary ▶ p.96

1 1 behaviour 2 accurately 3 possessions 4 warning 5 deceptive 6 disastrous

2 1 leave 2 violent 3 threaten 4 heavy 5 monitored 6 target 7 damage 8 warning

Vocabulary and Use of English ▶ p.97

1 1 since 2 during 3 for 4 over 5 country 6 scenery 7 wildlife 8 nature

2 1 D 2 A 3 A 4 B 5 C 6 A 7 B 8 C 9 A 10 D 11 B 12 C 13 A 14 C 15 A

Reading ▶ p.98

1 C 2 D 3 E 4 G 5 B 6 D 7 A 8 B 9 D 10 F 11 G 12 B 13 A 14 E

Grammar ▶ p.100

1
1. are said to be armed.
2. is thought to be innocent.
3. are reported to have been injured.
4. is believed to have entered the house through an open window.
5. are thought to be hiding in an empty building.
6. are expected to arrest three people.

2 1 being 2 be 3 have 4 ✓ 5 not 6 them
7 ✓ 8 it

3 1 is said that 2 are believed to be 3 are feared to be disappearing 4 is believed that
5 are thought to be 6 are said to be poisoning
7 is often claimed that 8 are reported to be dying
9 are believed to contain 10 are expected

Writing ▶ p.101

1.1 1 b) 2 b)

1.2 b)

1.3 b)

2.2 b), a), d), c)

2.3 Introduction
c), f)
The present situation
e)
Suggested action
a), b), d)

3 3

---

4 Sample answer:

To: The Head Teacher
From: Monica Serafini
Date: 10 July
Subject: How the school can help the environment

Introduction
This report is the result of a survey carried out among the students at the High School. The students were asked how they thought the school could do more to help the environment and what they would be prepared to do to help.

The present situation
Three main issues were identified.
• At the moment too many students come to school by car. This is wasteful and pollutes the atmosphere.
• The students are given too many worksheets by the teachers.
• The heating is usually set too high.

Suggested action
• A safe place to keep bicycles should be provided to encourage more students to cycle to school.
• To use less paper, books should be used instead of worksheets and recycling bins should be put around the school.
• The central heating and air conditioning systems should only be used when it is really necessary.

Conclusion
All these measures would help the environment locally and worldwide. Also if the school showed that it was concerned about this, it would help to educate the students in environmental awareness.

12 Careers

Vocabulary ▶ p.102

1 1 graduation 2 practical 3 promotion
4 advise 5 responsibility 6 voluntary

2 1 take on 2 going on 3 track down 4 find out
5 build up

3 1 join 2 get 3 spend 4 give 5 become
6 start

Grammar and Use of English ▶ p.102

1 1 were 2 would give 3 earned 4 would pay
5 spoke, could speak 6 hadn't fallen over
7 didn't have to 8 were 9 had listened
10 would come

2 1 was leaving   2 didn't tell   3 not to come
4 it if you telephoned   5 changed   6 to stay
7 study   8 did

3 1 I could speak   2 would rather you didn't   3
wishes he hadn't taken   4 only I had gone
5 is time you went   6 would rather study than go
7 I weren't so bad   8 only my boss wouldn't
9 is time they were leaving/left   10 wish you
were working

4 1 to   2 had   3 been   4 been   5 a   6 not

5 1 a   2 of   3 in   4 like   5 be   6 good/great
7 a   8 and   9 to   10 ended/finished   11 spent
12 been   13 have/need   14 the   15 any

Vocabulary ▶ p.104

1 1 for   2 in   3 on   4 for   5 on   6 out of

2 1 musician   2 highly   3 classical   4 soloist
5 competitive   6 performance

3.1 1 b)   2 e)   3 h)   4 d)   5 c)   6 g)   7 f)   8 a)

3.2 1 worthwhile   2 scruffy   3 dull   4 voluntary
5 exhausting   6 mature   7 challenging
8 thrilling

4 1 first-class   2 full-time   3 good-looking
4 left-handed   5 bad-tempered

Vocabulary and Use of English ▶ p.105

1 1 hard   2 lately   3 wide   4 hardly   5 late
6 widely

2 1 satisfaction   2 carefully   3 safety
4 competition   5 valuable   6 attentively
7 recommendations   8 highly   9 independence
10 memorable

Reading ▶ p.106

1 G   2 A   3 C   4 E   5 B   6 F

Grammar ▶ p.108

1 1 even if   2 despite   3 although   4 While   5
on the other hand   6 However   7 even though
8 but

2 1 because of   2 Furthermore   3 so   4 In spite of
the fact that   5 As well as

3 1 However   2 no   3 either   4 neither/nor
5 but   6 too   7 At   8 end   9 although
10 spite   11 because   12 Finally   13 well
14 though   15 at

Writing ▶ p.109

1.1 1 b)   2 b)

1.2 1 favour   2 against   3 both

2 a) X   b) ✓   c) X   d) ✓   e) ✓   f) X

4 Sample answer:

It is quite common for students to start working part-time while they are studying because they need their own money to pay for their studies and entertainment. The question is whether it is a good idea.

There are a lot of positive arguments for it. Firstly, students who are earning their own money can buy what they want. Moreover, they are independent and they gain valuable experience of real life.

On the other hand, students who work have less time to study or go out with friends. Hard work makes them tired or unhappy and it is not so good, for example, before an examination.

It is not enough to study and work. Young people need to enjoy life, discover new things, get to know other people, other cultures, learn languages and travel, so that they can survive in the real world.

To sum up, working while studying is a good idea but it is important to find the right balance and to choose work that is not too tiring.

Progress check 3 ▶ p.110

Grammar

1 1 would close   2 bought   3 could   4 had taken
5 work   6 paid   7 to go   8 had tried

2 1 had   2 discover   3 would have seen   4 would
you do   5 were   6 had been   7 take   8 saved

3 1 will have died   2 'm/am going to put   3 will be
living/will live   4 's/is thinking   5 'll/will be lying
6 was waiting   7 's/has been working   8 'd/had
seen   9 left   10 'll/will arrive/am going to arrive

4 1 couldn't have   2 must have   3 might/may have
4 were able   5 must   6 will be able
7 shouldn't have   8 didn't need to

5 1 someone   2 installed   3 had   4 ✓   5 to
6 been

6 1 are expected to rise considerably over the next
50 years
2 believed that dolphins are able to communicate
quite sophisticated messages.
3 thought that a cure for the common cold will be
found in the near future.
4 is said to be increasing.

Vocabulary

7.1

	Noun	Verb	Adjective
1	*information*	inform	*informative*
2	*fascination*	*fascinate*	fascinating
3	*understanding*	understand	*understanding/ understandable*
4	*discovery*	*discover*	discovered
5	solution	*solve*	*soluble*
6	*reduction*	reduce	*reduced*
7	thought	*think*	*thoughtful*

7.2 1 reduction 2 informative 3 thoughts
4 understandably 5 undiscovered

8 1 to 2 in 3 from 4 on 5 of 6 of 7 of
8 in 9 for 10 at

9 1 latest 2 sleep 3 due 4 updated 5 end
6 sum 7 Firstly 8 work

10 1 Despite 2 in spite 3 even if 4 Although
5 whereas